5-26-58

THE ESSENCE OF THE BIBLE

THE ESSENCE OF
THE BIBLE

by

Paul Claudel

PHILOSOPHICAL LIBRARY, INC.

NEW YORK

Translated from the French *J'aime la Bible* by Wade Baskin

Printed in the United States of America

Contents

1027432

THE ESSENCE OF THE BIBLE

CHAPTER I

My First Love: the Bible

Nature withheld from me the priceless gift of the artist's touch. And not being able to draw is a great handicap to me, for my mind teems with all sorts of images which require only a pencil for their expression. Take this one which haunts me: a mitered bishop clutching a cross and sailing along above the earth, not as the good Lord described in Psalms, riding a Seraph on his tours of inspection, but kneeling. Kneeling on a huge book opened in the middle with the pages unfolded like wings! His book is the Bible! I am no bishop, faithful to his duties as an inspector (*episcopus*), but since Providence has given me a flaming chariot for traveling through space and time, I should not refuse to put it to use. Kneeling!

The Bible is associated in my mind with the first stirrings of my heart and imagination. During earliest childhood, while learning to read under the guidance of the dear sisters of the Christian faith at Bar-le-Duc, I was fascinated by the big drawings placed in my hands, drawings depicting the life of the Lord. And later at the Lycée, my favorite preparatory subject was the Bible. The sacrifice of Abraham, the Flood, the betrothal of Rebecca, Jacob, Moses, Tobias, the punishment of Heliodorus, the Good Samaritan—so many magnifi-

1

cent pictures, and about each I can say but one thing: it was overwhelming. What a disappointment later on when I had to leave them for the Greeks, the Romans, and their successors!

And still later during the evening of an unforgettable Christmas Day in 1886, Providence must have intervened. On my table was a Bible, the gift of a Protestant friend to my sister Camille. I opened it, something that I had never done before, and opened it at two different places. The first was the part about Emmaus in St. Luke where the Lord, against the background of the oncoming night, revealed the secrets of the Old Testament to the burning hearts of His two companions. And the second was the sublime Chapter 8 of the Book of Proverbs, which is used as an Epistle at the Mass of the Immaculate Conception. Ah! I was quick to recognize the features of the Mother of God in the radiant figure which this passage evokes; I was quick to recognize the features of the Mother of God along with the inseparable features of the Church and divine Wisdom. Every female character in my later plays bore the imprint of this fascination.

What was I to do? The door to a new world had just been opened to me, but I still had an interest in this one. Both, according to the Scriptures, were created together—I mean as parts of one whole. Both make up the great catholic truth, called Heaven and Earth. How beautiful, heaven and earth! And God would not have created them without a purpose. Both make it possible for us to understand Him better and to love Him better. Jesus said: *I have overcome the world.* He did not overcome it by turning His back on it. He conquered it by surmounting it, by showing it the Cause—in Him, with Him, above Him. By carrying the Cause which He is with Him and emblazoning it on the cross. The Word is the last word. He did not come to leave the last word to the world.

And I who felt in my heart the great catholic calling, the

calling of the Universe, could do no better than embark on the discovery of the four cardinal points of the spiritual compass which had begun to spread its fledgling wings beneath me. For forty years my life was devoted to examining every horizon of the planet and every aspect of feeling. Then an idle circumstance caused me to understand that after a time of dispersion comes a time of unification. Then I realized that the Holy Scriptures are more than a vehicle, that they alone form a sublime edifice suited not only to worship but to residence, and that the whole world was made for the sole purpose of serving them as support and embellishment.

I was asked by a publisher, a man named Pichon, to write a preface to a new edition of the Book of Revelation which he was preparing. I was not long in rejecting his request. The Book of St. John, which I had reread many times—despite its flashing beauty and the strange sweetness that emanates from it—had always repelled me by its violence, by the uncomfortable place that it occupies between heaven and earth, and by the challenges that it constantly hurls at the intelligence of the reader. *Who hath ears to hear let him hear.* I did not understand. I refused to yield to loose historical interpretations. Yet my esteem for the word of God made me believe that His word should not be restricted to any actual event.

Though I had brushed aside the indiscreet solicitor, I had not put an end to his proposal. Night and day, it gave me no rest. I was sixty and not busy; I was forever through with such works as *L'ôtage* and *Le soulier de satin;* and I knew that *Tête d'or* had drawn the final balance sheet for all the *Ysès* and *Prouhèzes*. I had enough time, and curiosity focused my interest on the Book of Revelation. Why not give it a try? It would be a matter of a few days, a few weeks at most. . . .

I was sixty at that time, as I said, and now I am past eighty-three. In all probability, only the grave will put an end to the bold and fascinating investigation in which I became engaged through an endless chain of questions and challenges which I was powerless to evade. *Lord, I have loved the habitation of Thy house,* says a psalm. What house can compare with the Scriptures which are the temple of divine thought? And not only in beauty, but in what I call ultimate beauty, the substance of beauty which is meaning.

The Book of Revelation, I was soon to find out, has precisely the meaning that it derives from and gives to the Scriptures as seen in their full context, just as a river acquires its meaning, after successive rivulets and many meanderings, through the horizon into which it empties. The Book of Revelation searches everywhere for the drops found in what Job called the divine *stream of brooks,* and gives them weight, slope and direction. Not one verse fails to contain a reference or allusion—and sometimes multiple ones—to a source of the past and to provide the link between alpha and omega. At that time, I no longer thought of the Bible as a confused mass of unrelated and, if you will, picturesque documents hooked together by prophetic insights; I looked upon it rather as a self-contained architectural marvel and as a monumental volume pregnant with meaning and bound with matchless artistry. Directly under my eyes was the city, *harmoniously united,* mentioned in Psalm 119. An astounding city, a living city wherein stability does not exclude movement and wherein the past never stops obeying the future. An architectural drama whose author, the same through I know not how many centuries, is responsible for the theater, the lines and the actors as well as the action. Finally I was granted an overall view, an *intelligible* view, something resembling an *a posteriori* view, of the Promised Land. How could I tear my attention away from it?

The Bible is made up of two collections of books known as *Testaments,* the Old Testament and the New Testament. A testament is in the legal sense the act through which a person states his will and disposes of his belongings before his death. *Act* means that someone who was but no longer is there continues still to act on us through writing, to reveal himself, to express himself to us, to hand us his belongings in accordance with certain conditions which he outlines. The difference is this: the human testament belongs to someone who has ceased to exist and has been separated for all time from his legacy. God's testament belongs to someone who always stands beside His will and is always present in the form of the good things which he provides for us. For in short, the good things which he provides for us as owners, owners with the right to *use* and *abuse* as defined by Roman law, are none other than God Himself. We might say that through His absence He invests us with His presence.

God's written, authenticated legacy to us was none other than His Son, *the beloved Son,* says the Gospel, *in whom He was well pleased.* Indeed, He alone was the legitimate heir to all that belonged to His Father by birthright, not by usurpation.

Such a legacy could be bequeathed only by the Father and inherited only by the Son. The Old Testament was the legacy of everything which worked, across the centuries and until its subsequent realization through the merits of Christ, toward its climax in the Incarnation, the Holy Virgin. And the New Testament was the dispensation of this long-awaited fruit through sacraments. The Righteousness of the Virgin's breast was inspired by Mercy. Everything happened at the same time. Grace rained down from the height of the cross and under its beneficent influence the earth engendered its Saviour.

And then the world had meaning. No longer did it move aimlessly about. No longer was it an unintelligible chaos. It had come from somewhere and it was going somewhere. And we ourselves, to the extent that we share in its general meaning and act individually in its general movement, have meaning; our life, the movement which animates us from the cradle to the grave, acquires meaning and dignity. The psalmist compares this movement to the writer's pen which moves along, leaving behind a lasting meaning.

The Word had to have a language and vocabulary of its own in order to communicate with us and draw up a letter of instructions which we could understand. Its vocabulary was not made by human hands and did not consist of expressions coined by men. Its vocabulary was the inexhaustible repertory of the Creator's meaningful images: the whole of Creation. Someone came to liberate Creation from Vanity, for it is written that Creation *was its unwilling subject*. Behold the unwilling subject, like a mute creature whose tongue is loosed and who has something to say. Pascal confides to us that the *eternal silence of infinite space terrifies him*. Silence! He must have been a bad listener! Against this, the psalmist tells us that every noise in the world, every vocal sound conveys to him the first part of the Hebrew word for Father, *Abba!* I mean that, coming from God, every sound continues its trajectory solely to find in Him its end, to carry to something that is the confession of something that is not, to set before Him the sight of continuing preference by not ceasing to be reborn in order to be born anew. The whole vocabulary of the Scriptures consists only of concrete terms, which are real words and images whose meanings are brought out by their associations. These divine images ask only to consummate a sacrifice of significations at His feet.

The world is more than a vocabulary. From it we derive our whole system of usage. Philosophy teaches us to divide grammar into substantives, which are things and beings, adjectives which are qualities, verbs which are action, adverbs which qualify action, and moods and tenses indicating action and reaction. Nature found the means to make herself understood not only to our ears but also to our minds. She speaks.

She does not soliloquize like an idiot. She speaks of someone and she speaks to someone. And we have the Bible to
compel us to listen and to understand what she brings into
existence before our very eyes—the substance of her speech
and art. This is summed up in one word: serve. She serves.
She serves in both senses of the word. First, she honors her
Creator. Second, she serves him. Not only in an officiating
capacity, but as a servant. She serves him in the administra-
tion of his chattels. From the very first lines of Genesis, the
Scriptures tell us that she is good and that she is good for
something. Everything that God created is good for something. None of God's creatures can get along without all the
others. From weather maps we learn that the whole planet
is affected by the weather of our locality. And at the same
time much bad literature has been written about the basic
law of nature which states that creatures can not live without
each other and that they love each other so much that they
devour each other. We can see in this law of nature a primitive
form of communion, one that will one day yield to a higher
form. And rather than become upset, we should praise God
for giving each little creature the right food at the opportune
time.

The spectacle of nature helps us to understand the
drunkenness and enthusiasm of a David in contrast to all
the bitter and sneering Michols. It is not enough to say that
he sings, cries, shouts, dances with joy and calls on every
creature to help him say thanks! Ah! The sorrowful, hopeless mood of pagan literature has disappeared, now that we
have the good Lord with us! We have the world which He
made and which asks only to serve Him in some way. The
visible world and, above the visible world—would you believe it?—an invisible world which is even more wonderful.
Above the world of effects, the world of causes; above the
world of Law, that of Providence; above time, events; and
beyond immediacy, history. The greater part of the Scrip-

tures is devoted to the second aspect of God's stewardship of
men.

I hear the objection. True, there are times when God's
work seems complete or, to use an expression from *Ecclesiasticus,* when it fills our senses like the Euphrates, and we feel
in complete harmony with it. It can even be said that the
purer a heart, the farther a mind reaches out and penetrates
and the more wonder and thanksgiving flood the mind. This
is the attitude of contemplation. We Westerners find it wanting. We do not become so absorbed in the present as to confuse it with eternity. We must live; we are conscious of a duty
to fulfill, of something to pursue, of a certain logical obligation to our roles in the play. Each step that we take and each
glance that we cast around us puts us in contact with evil,
with suffering, with sin, with the most offensive shapes. And
then with new intensity there rises within us the irradicable
question of old: If God is good, and if He is omnipotent,
why all this?

The Church, far from ignoring the question, introduced
it—I was about to say incorporated it—in its liturgy in the
most daring and virulent form that it has ever had. Each year
the Mass of the Dead again reminds us of the almost blasphemous defense of Hus: *Do not condemn me; shew me
wherefore thou contendest with me. Oh that my grief were
thoroughly weighed and my calamity laid in the balances
together! Behold, I cry out of wrong, but I am not heard: I
cry aloud, but there is no judgment. But how should man be
just with God? If he will contend with Him, he cannot answer Him one or a thousand. For He is not a man, as I am,
that I should answer Him, and we should come together in
judgment. Who is he that will plead with me? For now, if I
hold my tongue, I shall give up the ghost. Withdraw Thine
hand far from me, and let not Thy dread make me afraid.
Then call Thou, and I will answer; or let me speak, and
answer Thou me. Wherefore hidest Thou Thy face, and*

*holdest me for Thine enemy? Is it good unto Thee that thou
shouldest oppress, that Thou shouldest despise the work of
Thine hands, and shine upon the counsel of the wicked?
That Thou enquirest after mine iniquity, and searchest after
my sin? Thou knowest that I am not wicked; and there is
none that can deliver me out of Thine hand.*

God did not condemn Job for his enraged petition. Not in
the least. On the contrary, He laid the blame on Job's friends
—who undertook to defend the Creator by using irrelevant
arguments; He blamed them to the extent that he refused
to pardon them until Job interceded for them. *Who is this
that darkeneth counsel by words without knowledge? Qui
sunt isti involventes sententias in sermonibus imperitis?* And
then the Lord, placing his mouth near his servant's ear,
whispered mysteries.

The Book of Job is a part of the oldest collection of Biblical literature. At the opposite end of a literary route that
wound through the centuries, another Job appeared. But this
one was much sadder; He was a much more perfect summary
of all that human destiny could reveal, not only about physical and moral suffering but about injustice which is not accidental but implicit. We have reached and entered Gethsemane. This is not the story of a rich proprietor's loss of his
estate, of a family's loss of its children, and of flesh and bone
being seized upon by a blind, ignorant enemy. This is Gethsemane, where God was made man. God took upon himself
all the horror of mankind. Behold, Old Job! You asked for
justice and here He is in answer to your plea. You asked him
to appear as an equal. He has done that. What have you to
say? Is He sufficiently shorn of divinity? You would search in
vain for something more naked, more vulnerable. Job had
friends who, clumsily to be sure, but sincerely, took an interest in his fate. This One also had friends whom He had
nourished for three years on His inmost thought and feelings, and, it can even be said, on His flesh and blood. They

were snoring there on the ground, and as soon as they awoke from their stupor, they fled. One of them, the dearest one, denied Him, and another betrayed Him for money. In the name of the very law which He himself gave to men, He was solemnly accused, judged, condemned, excommunicated, executed. The startled Angels looked upon the Creator of the world, held captive and defenseless by his adversary.

What adversary? The one we saw rise up in the first verses of the Book of Job, in the first chapters of the Book of Genesis; this is the one of old who emerged from eternity to set time in motion. Would he prevail? Certainly the Devil surrendered to justice when he fled from love. But all the same, there is nothing that exists outside God, that continues outside God, that no longer serves God, that is no longer of service to God. All of God's work had to make adjustments for a falsifier.

That could not be tolerated. The good Lord owed it to Himself to put an end to the scandal. I have already mentioned the reverent tears which the sight of His immovableness draws from us. It is hard to describe those evoked by His actions as we watch Him rise up like a giant to save His injured work. His task was not to suppress evil but to find the means of making it serve Him, in order that at His name *every knee should bend, of things in heaven, and things in earth, and things under the earth.*

That was the accomplishment of the marvelous invention revealed to us through the Scriptures, from the first to the last. What a subject! Beside it, what are all man-made epics? It is a true testament, the memoirs of someone who is the central figure of his narrative.

A gripping narrative, and not only of the past, not of something fancied, but of something real, something that continues, closely tied to the plot of our own existence; a drama lived, I would say, not so much by us as through Him, just as the actors of the Old Testament lived through Him.

We have heard Man complain of his fate through the mouth
of Job, of his brief career leading from the cradle to the grave
through suffering, ignorance and sin. This is the wretched
and contrite fate which God, the Perfect One, the incom-
municable Being, chose to take upon Himself as the lowliest and most reviled of men (these are the very words used in
the Scriptures). He asked a creature like us to share her
heart with Him. He needed the creature, and thanks to her,
a matchless Someone rose up in the middle of the Story and
declared that he was not only the son of Man but the son of
God. But such matchless grace was even greater than is apparent. We were needed! God needed us! He drew us to
Adam *with bands of love.* And through His prophet, He
tells us: *I will betroth thee unto Me in Righteousness.*

In Righteousness? How?

God is the sole end of man. Why should he not be the sole
end of Himself? Incarnation and redemption are boundless
acts through which man has benefited, but the final aim of
the Son and of the Father was one and the same: to repair
the damage done to the Father, to restore His ruined work—
ruined not only by the original sin of man, but by the primordial revolt of Satan. It is astounding and overwhelming
to think that for this work He needed us and continues to
need us. Whence the incomparable dignity of the Holy Virgin above and beyond all the other Saints. And we, too, according to our place in time and our calling in the Church,
are asked to help God! We were granted this favor! The poor
man whom we heard moaning a moment ago, howling in
despair from his dunghill—God did not come to his rescue
but called on Job to rescue Him.

Somewhere St. Paul tells us that *death is swallowed up in
victory.* Similarly, it might be said that evil was swallowed
up in the cure, that sin was swallowed up in expiation and
that transgression was swallowed up in sacrifice. That is why
the Apostle tells us that Christ was *crucified . . . that the*

body of sin might be destroyed (*Romans 6:6*). The Savior
acts on Mankind as a revulsion, drawing toward Himself all
of the hostile and sorrowful elements and blending them
into an effective remedy which He offers to the Creator. Now
the demon can go to the devil! Anything which he can do or
imagine is just that much more water poured over the mill of
Christ. Indeed, I believe St. Ignatius of Antioch is the one
who mentions the machine of Christ, *machina Christi.* Since
it was carried up Calvary this machine has not stopped run-
ning; it is exactly like the one that trickles down on our altars
daily. It is the heart which He asked of the Holy Virgin and
which we now share with Him. So it is that the Reaper of
Chapter 63 of Isaiah tramples underfoot the constantly renewed vintage of our sufferings and sins.

*   *   *

The existence or actual presence of God, as He emerged
in the first pages of the Scriptures, gave meaning to nature.
When He states that His work is good, the Creator means
two things. First, His work, since it has the beauty that blends
with existence only through Him, holds in reserve, as from
cause to effect, an indicative power. The Buddhists believe
that the world is an *illusion,* but Genesis teaches us that it is
an *allusion.* Second, we learn that nature is not only good,
but that it is good for something; that it serves; that it is designed for a purpose and serves a purpose; and that its purpose is to honor its Creator by perpetuating itself.

And then, sprung from a primordial drama which was not
fully resolved until the last pages of the Book of Revelation,
emerged man, the agent of restoration who, after having
added his own betrayal to Satan's, gave a linear direction to
time across the recurrent ceremony of the years. The Story
began. It began through its end. It began from the starting
point of the cross which had already been planted on Calvary

and which was to draw to it, from constantly widening horizons, men, nations and events. Everything becomes clearer in the Story as in nature through its relationship to God. Everything in nature is a symbol and everything that happens is a parable. This is the truth that the Lord tried to bring to our attention by making us see and think about the supreme Gesture, the appearance of His Son. In Him we see that every expectation of Man was fulfilled. Every generation comes in turn to pay tribute to Him and to receive orders from Him through His Word. *My Father worketh hitherto,* said the Savior, *and I work.* The Bible is the outline of His work; as such, it deserves to be called the Story of Jesus, though the title is properly restricted to the events leading from the Messianic preparation to its fulfilment.

The Story of Jesus is an inspired story. Both the narrative and the events that comprise its substance are inspired. Wholly inspired, according to what we are told by St. Paul, the infallible teacher. *Inspired*—I should prefer to say "breathed in"—through the incarnate Word which finally came as the intelligible expression of a long-standing desire. God used speech to tell about Himself and, according to the unanimous belief of the ancient Church Fathers, He is not absent, either directly or indirectly, from any part of His Writ. We must heed the injunction that comes from Heaven: *This is My well-beloved Son; hear ye Him.* Hear means that we must never turn away from His intention or stop giving our attention to the intention and meaning of the mouth of Christ who is speaking. For Christ speaks in order to enter His deposition before the tribunal of Mankind.

All I am doing here is conforming to the instructions of St. Paul, who wrote at the beginning of his Epistle to the Hebrews: *God who at sundry times and in divers manners spake in time past unto the fathers by the prophets, hath in these last days spoken unto us by his Son, whom He hath appointed heir of all things, by whom also he made the worlds.* This capital text shows us the whole of Creation, from one point in time to the next, pregnant with meaning; the writer's pen animates all its scattered words by linking them together and giving them meaning. A sentence is made, so to speak, of transient words which give up or bequeath their particular values to the sentence and become no more than the substance of its form. But God is more than a grammarian; He is an artist; He is a poet skilled in all the resources of discourse; as He moves along, He asks of things and events—as a ray interpreted through all angles of incidence and refraction—an appropriate testimonial, *multifariam multisque modis,* in many circumstances and in many ways. This means that aside from Messianic texts as such, which contemporary critics and translators are making every effort to diminish in number and importance, the Scriptures contain many allusions and faint echoes to delight hearts and ears made sensitive by love. For God was willing to confide many things to us only through whispers. From this point of view, nothing can ever replace our matchless Vulgate. All else is dull, flat, cold and coarse by contrast—like Virgil translated by a fourth-year student.

God is the meaning of the Scriptures. Men and events are there to give testimony concerning God; God is not there to give testimony for men and their history or to satisfy the itchings of their curiosities. One would think so, however, to judge by voluminous and vacuous exegetic literature which aims only at the how and not at the why, and which results only in illusions and conjectures which destroy each other. Without God's meaning, the Bible is meaningless.

I am not a scholar or a doctor of divinity. I am only a poet. But what is the Bible if not a vast poem? The total lack of any kind of poetic feeling, or of the sensitivity of the soul which the Bible itself classes as *understanding,* is no basis for granting a license for the study of the Scriptures. Every page of the Book of Isaiah bids us lift up our eyes. We can lift up our eyes only if we take our noses off the ground. In any event, poet or not, I am a Christian determined to let no one deprive me, under technical pretexts, of any part of the vast heritage of the Church, for the Christian liturgy has left on my tongue an irradicable taste for this heritage. I gain confidence from the fact that the great lady known as Theology—or so it would seem if I am to believe her most eloquent servant, the great Bossuet—stands beside poetry and liturgy. I find this passage in Bossuet's admirable attempt to confute the heretic Richard Simon: *We should certainly be in a woeful condition if to defend truth and the legitimate interpretation of the Scriptures we were at the mercy of the Hebraists and Hellenists who generally show such weak reasoning in all things.*

We have just seen the magnitude of the contribution of the idea of God to the spectacle of nature. Indeed, Creation could not dispense with its Creator. It wanted to speak and managed to speak. It spoke to someone about something. Whether interpreted as a poem or as a scientific treatise, Creation spoke. Isolated terms entered into communication with each other and were resolved into meaning. Everywhere rich analogy was the instrument of discovery.

We also saw that there is no being, nothing, however lowly, which does not in some humble way bear the imprint of God. In man, the imprint is an image. It is a conscious and active image. *Ye are gods,* a psalm tells us. Something like a vice-God. *I have made thee a God to Pharaoh,* said the Lord to Moses. What an honor and what a responsibility! It follows that the Commandment which warns us *not to take the name of the Lord in vain* refers to something other than oaths and blasphemies. We are the images of God; we stand for Him and act for Him in all our deeds and movements. It is through Him that we are all fathers, for St. Paul advises us that *we are the children of God, and if children, then heirs.* It is through Him also that we are judges. We are the holders of His property. We are the investigators, the interpreters, the attorneys, the actors, the defendants, the assessors of His Will. And St. Peter adds that we are His priests and that no Christian is denied a certain priestly character—priests because guardians of His temples.

But one important side of our likeness and kinship to God stands out. St. John tells us that *God is love*. On the frontispiece of divine Law is inscribed the motto: THOU SHALT LOVE. *Thou shalt love the Lord thy God with all thine heart, and with all thy soul, and with all thy might.* You must love Him, not only for Himself, but through His works which are in His image and which are described as *good,* good for Him.

Love springs from need. We know that our need can be satisfied only by the fixed being who stands apart from us. Starved by the effect, we cleave to the cause. That is why even the fiercest animals love the hand that feeds them. Similarly, among men the most elemental and natural virtue is the gratitude that makes us responsive to our parents and benefactors and binds us to them. Gratitude is a magnificent word. It suggests that the key to the heart, to that within us which makes us what we are, to the person that we are, is the good that we are capable of doing for each other. That is why it would seem possible for us to love God by exerting our minds and wills only slightly if not thwarted by original sin. "How beautiful it is!" say the artist and the sage, made delirious by the spectacle of the wonderful world in which they were placed. And any living being can add: "How good it is!" Yes, we have an endless catalogue of grievances and are exposed to all sorts of contradictions. But a little reflection shows us that only good is basic, since it blends with being; evil is always accidental, episodical and unexpected. Evil is a misdeed that catches up with us, as we say colloquially, and which the scholastic adage put in this way: *Bonum ex integra*

causa, salum ex quocumque defectu. The Old Testament is
the bulging repository of all of God's favors. In it is stored
every favor which, from the beginning the Creator has been
obliged to hold under the nose of the brutish creature who
forgets his maker. In this way God also reminds us that suffering has a fairly obvious, though not directly comprehensi-
ble, link with sin. And finally, these favors show that our
Creator has not run away, but that He is here, right beside
us; that He is good, swift with mercy, as attested by countless examples, and prompt to make amends when disturbances result from the violation of the rules which through
His goodness He asked and counseled us to observe for our
own good rather than at His command.

That is the order of nature, of Law, of Righteousness. As
the crowning touch the author of all these favors added Himself, raising one scale of the balance to heaven and plunging
the other down to hell. How heartily we should repeat the
words of praise which the *Gloria* of the Mass brings to our
lips every day!

But beside Righteousness stands Grace. All the thoughts
and feelings that might be expected to enter into love, but
not love. The mind has a ready answer for a question, but
the heart can only reply in the language of small children:
because He was and because I was: *Gratia pro gratia,* as St.
John tells us. We in turn respond to Grace freely and openly.
God seeded the world with His likeness and, outranking all
else by far, with the most vital mystery of His Being, the
production of offspring. That, says St. Paul, is a *great sacrament, the supreme sacrament, magnum sacramentum.* And
from the first pages of the history of Mankind onward, we
see the Creator's seal affixed to its organ, our virility. God
needed a root in the innermost part of Mankind, and He
asked it of the sacred union between man and woman. Of
this union it is said that *therefore shall a man leave his father
and his mother, and shall cleave unto his wife: and they*

shall be one flesh in order that they may use one heart to be two.

And abruptly I am forced to remember. *Hearken, O daughter . . .* is a verse from the celebrated Psalm 45, which has always been thought by the Church to apply to the Holy Virgin. *Hearken, O daughter, and consider, and incline thy ear; forget also thy people and thy father's house; so shall the King greatly desire thy beauty, for He is thy Lord; and worship thou Him.* He Himself is speaking! Truly He delights in being with the children of man, and truly Job's divine *stream of brooks,* seeks but a simple "yes" in answer to this plea: *My son, my daughter, give me thy heart. I live,* said St. Paul, *yet not I, but Christ liveth in Me.*

In the beginning God made a pact with His creature. He promised to keep regular appointments. The Book of Genesis tells us that as He placed the fishes in the sea and man himself in the mire, He appeared, *epiphané,* and gradually revealed Himself to succeeding generations. The Canticle of Simeon tells us that He slowly made Himself manifest in order that we might discover our own hearts, that is, our latent potentialities. Through the solicitation of a face gradually coming into full view, the intrinsically sacred and good appetite which we share with the animals culminates gloriously in such angelic personages as St. Francis and St. Theresa. *The Lord hath appeared of old, saying, Yea I have loved thee with an everlasting love,* Jeremiah tells us, *therefore with loving kindness have I drawn thee.*

The Scriptures spell out the tender teaching of Grace line by line. To tell us to love God and to explain the reason is not enough; they teach us how. They show us, not drawings like those which the dear sisters of Bar-le-Duc once showed me, but facts about living men and women—enduring because they are typical.

Gradually there comes to light the true nature of the pact

concluded with the people whom He chose to prepare for
Him the flesh of His Son: it is an exemplary pact, an oath
sworn to by both parties, like a nuptial vow. Every violation
acquires heart-rending power. It is not only deceitful, but
adulterous. We not only do wrong; we wrong someone.
Popule meus, we hear sung on Good Friday, *quid feci tibi
et in quo contristavi te?*

The wedding day, the long awaited wedding day, has
come, and just as Jerusalem reaches the height of its splen-
dor, in the shadow of the Temple in which the Holy Ghost
resides, the epithalamium bursts forth. It is the *Song of
Songs,* perhaps the most important book of the Bible with
the exception of the Book of Job. The terrible Sinaitic Yahweh
had appeared in lightening and in earthquakes but here a
woman *ravished His heart with one of her eyes, with one
chain of her neck.* He became the lover, the beloved. She led
Him into her mother's house where she prepared for Him the
cup which He was to have ample time to savor at Gethsemane
and on Calvary. And He in turn taught her something which
triumphs over death and which is beyond death; it is priceless in comparison with all else, including the surrender of
body and substance.

From that point on, the Bible is a love story. It appeals to
the tenderest and most innocent and profound feelings of
the human heart; it is more moving than the most frequently
read novels of any country. The Mankind of woman was
stirring in the guise of Rebecca and Ruth and strong under
the guise of Dalila and Bethsheba; now it was a father send-
ing his son into deepest Asia to tear Mankind away from
demons and to hold out his hand; it was the King of the
Universe sharing his sceptre until a besieged town should
trust him and hand over a victorious sword. What goodness
on the part of the Bridegroom, and, on the part of the Bride,
alas, what frivolity, what madness and, to answer an ever
ready objection, what unwearied treachery! We hear from

Ezekiel the complaint of a lover who is at the same time a father. He begins by describing human wretchedness, reminding us of Job. Man was a pitiful creature who traced his origin to far from illustrious crossings, a pagan whom no-one bothered to clean with salt and wrap in swaddling-cloths when he emerged from his mother's womb. He was cast out stark naked on the earth, like the poor little Chinese girls whom I have seen rolled in a mat and abandoned on vacant lots to the teeth of dogs and swine. *And when I passed by thee, and saw thee polluted in thine own blood, I said unto thee when thou wast in thy blood, Live; yea, I said unto thee when thou wast in thy blood, Live. I have caused thee to multiply as the bud of the field, and thou hast increased and waxen great, and thou art come to excellent ornaments: thy breasts are fashioned, and thine hair is grown, whereas thou wast naked and bare. Now when I passed thee, and looked upon thee, behold, thy time was the time of love; and I spread my skirt over thee, and covered thy nakedness; yea, I sware unto thee, saith the Lord God, and thou becamest mine. Then I washed thee with water, yea, I throughly washed away thy blood from thee, and I anointed thee with oil. I clothed thee also with broidered work, and shod thee with badgers' skin, and I girded thee about with fine linen, and I covered thee with silk. I decked thee also with ornaments, and I put bracelets upon thy hands, and a chain on thy neck* (here the allusion is to the Commandments which are both our shackles and our glory). *And I put a jewel on thy forehead, and earrings in thine ears, and a beautiful crown upon thine head. Thus wast thou decked with gold and silver, and thy raiment was of fine linen, and silk, and broidered work; thou didst eat fine flour, and honey, and oil: and thou wast exceedingly beautiful, and thou didst prosper into a kingdom. And thy renown went forth among the heathen for thy beauty: for it was perfect through my comeliness, which I had put upon thee, saith the Lord God.*

And how did this admirable creature thank her benefactor? I leave the task of enlightenment to Latin: *Habens fiduciam in pulchritudine tua, fornicata es in nomine tue*—you gave yourself to every passerby, to the advocates of notions in fashion for a day and for an hour, in the name of *thine own beauty*, forgetting the name of God, the sacred name which so many people today recall only to curse.

But from the depths of this abasement the voice of another prophet invited the unfortunate creature to rise up. *Shake thyself from the dust, loose thyself from the bands of thy neck, O captive daughter of Zion! Awake, awake; put on thy beautiful garments. See the throne of glory that was established of old!* Up to this point we were in the domain of allegory. Ezekiel's prostitute typifies Judah in much the same way as the statues of the Place de la Concorde typify French cities. Now the limits of poetry, however exalted, are removed and the horizon takes on the hues of a still more sublime theology. The Book of Deuteronomy commands us to love God, but man was not long in perceiving his powerlessness to carry out the commandment all alone: for his answer he needed nothing less than the whole Universe for which he is responsible. *I will praise thee*, says the psalmist, *in the Temple*. Man understood that he was capable of fulfilling his duty to God only in the Temple. *Thou art all fair, my love*, says the Song of Songs, meaning that she is fair only because she is complete. And we read a little further on that in Baal-hamon, "that which hath people," *the Peacemaker had a vineyard*. People? Not just the offspring of Jacob. *The place is too straight for me*, cried the prophet, *fac mihi spatium, give place to me!* And Psalm 87 gloriously proclaims: *I will make mention of Rahab and Babylon to them that know me: behold Philistia, and Tyre, with Ethiopia; this man was born there. And of Zion it shall be said, This and that man was born in her: and the highest Himself shall establish her.*

This is where the Old Testament stops and the New begins. Yahweh's beloved, though not necessarily complete, was one. *Una est amica mea,* says the Song. In the name of the whole Universe there had to be someone capable of keeping a promise, someone reliable, someone capable of answering the solemn question put by God as a bridegroom to his bride in the name of the whole Universe and in the name of all the generations of man until the end of the centuries! The proposal made, there had to be someone capable of bringing it to fruition inside her body. *Shall I bring to the birth and not cause to bring forth, and shut the womb? saith thy God.*

There, between the two Testaments, between heaven and earth, stands the ark of the covenant which St. John placed in the center of his Revelation.

*   *   *

Because God was made man, because He took an *interest,* as they say commercially, in Mankind, because He brought Mankind everything that He had as a dowry, and because He shared His own name with Mankind—*thou shalt call me Ishi, my husband,* said the prophet Hosea, *and shalt call me no more Baali*—the Spirit that He sent to us at Pentecost will not fly away to parts unknown and the shepherd will not desert his flock. Certainly not! *I will not leave you comfortless* and *I am with thee until the consummation of the centuries* are the last words of His Testament. Besides, through the institution of the Eucharist He found the means to live with us in a more immediate and substantial way than during His actual sojourn. *He who made the generations,* as St. Paul said, and who caused the Story to begin, as we saw, will not henceforth absent Himself from the needs of Mankind. He will still be there as the Guide and Shepherd to lead the flock which now includes not only Abraham's offspring, but all offspring from the time of Adam until the climactic hour of the second birth.

We can see the outlines of the future, not by climbing the vertiginous height of the Apocalypse, but by falling back to the beginning of time and making use of the prophetic documents.

My Father works and I too, I work until this day. God made man and made man in the Church which, according to St. Paul, is His own body. This work can be studied from two points of view, that of expression and that of unity.

Behold, at the dawn of each new year old Simeon repeats, *this child is sent that the thoughts of many hearts may be revealed.* Only through an enigmatic stroke do many people realize at times the existence of this unknown man, this imprisoned personage—*the Kingdom of heaven is in us,* say the Gospels. I am not alive unless I know why I live, and we should never know if Christ had not come to tell us, and if the Someone who gave us being had not come to give our lives a purpose and meaning.

Chapter 63 of Isaiah depicts a vintager who tirelessly treads underfoot the ever renewed bed of grapes which he is to convert into wine. And we know that the eternal worker is none other than our Savior. *They have no wine,* the Holy Virgin told Him. His task is to provide it for them. His task is to break the hard shell of our hearts, to squeeze out what is inside them, and to bring into communion all their accumulated selfishness: Shakespeare spoke of *the milk of human kindness* and his metaphor is striking. But we might also speak of *the wine of human kindness. Vae soli,* says the Book of Ecclesiastes, through charity which is the close, piercing contact sought and furnished by fellow-creatures, our veins are filled as if by fermentation with the vital, energizing heat from all our organic metabolisms. Nothing short of God, nothing short of the winepress of the cross, nothing short of the *machina Christi* was needed to extract something liquid and something burning, something living and enlivening from the hard, dry shell of the hearts of pagans, who are, as we learn from the Epistle to the Romans, heartless, merciless and untractable. Even today we need not search far to find those whom the description fits. But the two feet which are regularly raised and lowered suggest the beating of the heart. For the heart is the perpetual vintager of the body. And since the Church is the body of Christ, He is its heart. This is not a heart made of plaster or of bread crumbs but a heart perpetually at work; it is constantly engaged in the blissful vintage of the Peacemaker's Vineyard. The Bible tells us that blood is the vehicle of the soul and that God *will require it at the hand of every beast,* and from us, powerful animals that we are, as a guarantee of dispensation. The heart has a dual function, according to physiologists; as it draws carbon dioxide to it through the veins, it sends out oxygen through the arteries, using one to feed the other after it has been consumed on the altar of the central organ. And we can compare the dual complementary function of purification and revival to that of Christ in His Church which draws to Him all that is dark and destructible in Mankind and converts it into heat and light.

This is the process of inner unity and acquisition; it is the inner form of charity. This is the sense in which Christ, surrounded by His apostles at the Last Supper, asked His Father *that they may be one as We are one.* But beside the evangelizing of the Kingdom of heaven which is within us, there is that of the Kingdom of heaven which is outside us. The angel of the Nativity declared to the shepherds that he was announcing to them a great joy *which shall be to all people.* And the Savior Himself said that *when He arose, he would draw all men to Him.* He left as His most important command to His disciples the preaching of the gospel *to every creature,* to whom he came to give a purpose. He is the touchstone who makes two things into one; unity can be achieved through Him, but there is no unity outside Him. Anything that is not in His likeness passes away. In Him all

human nature, without distinction as to origin or race, finds
fulfilment. He is adapted to all our senses and meets all the
needs of our natures. According to the Book of Proverbs, He
fills all our senses like the Euphrates. It would be futile for
any tribe to attempt to do away with Him or to confiscate
what Isaiah calls *the sounding of His bowels.* And from all
sides voices cry out: *Doubtless thou art our father, though
Abraham be ignorant of us and Israel acknowledge us not;
thou, O Lord, art our Father, our Redeemer; Thy name is from
everlasting.* After mentioning Ephraim and Judah, Psalm 60
continues: *Moab is my washpot; over Edom will I cast out my
shoe; Philistia, triumph thou because of me. Who will bring
me into the strong city?* Across the iron curtain and into the
heart of the pagan desert? Who will lead thee, Lord? This is
the task set aside for Thy catholic and apostolic Church; this
is the duty of the woman described by St. John—the woman
who stood crying in the sunlight. In the pagan Cornelius'
house, St. Peter, the first pope, was called upon to climb
higher, that is, to enlarge his horizon. *Kill and eat,* said the
celestial messenger, thus ending the legal distinction between pure and impure animals. But another interpretation
is possible. The animals stand for the different races of men;
the Head of the Church is ordered to assimilate them after
he has used baptismal waters to destroy whatever invites destruction. Indeed, everything that can be absorbed into the
body of Christ is nourishment for the Church. All artificial
barriers which His enemy seeks constantly to erect—classes,
castes, iron curtains, racial prejudices, chauvinistic feelings—
are dissipated by the luminous breath of the Church. Add to
this view the prophetic enthusiasm of the last chapters of the
Book of Isaiah;

*Arise, shine; for thy light is come, Jerusalem, and the glory
of the Lord is risen upon thee. For, behold, the darkness shall
cover the earth, and gross darkness the people: but the Lord
shall arise upon thee, and His glory shall be seen upon thee.*

And the Gentiles shall come to thy light, and kings to the brightness of thy rising. Lift up thine eyes round about and see: all they gather themselves together, they come to thee: thy sons shall come from far, and thy daughters shall be nursed at thy side. Then thou shalt see, and flow, together, and thine heart shall fear, and be enlarged; because the abundance of the sea shall be converted unto thee, the forces of the Gentiles shall come unto thee. The multitude of camels shall cover thee. . . .* Do you know what these long-necked, two-humped camels suggest to me? A living, four-footed horizon! *The multitude of camels shall cover thee,* as if to say a multitude of horizons. Like the Magi, *the dromedaries of Midian and Ephah and all they from Sheba shall come: they shall shew forth the praises of the Lord. Surely the Isles shall wait for Me, and the ships of Tarshish first, to bring thy sons from far, unto the name of the Lord thy God. And the sons of strangers shall build up thy walls. Thy gates shall be open continually, that men may bring unto thee the forces of the Gentiles—from Africa, from Italy, from Libya, from Greece, all sorts of people who have never heard of Me. And they shall announce My glory to the gentiles who will bring to us their brothers from all over the world as an offering to the Lord: on horses, in carriages, in ships! All sorts of sons and daughters astride their shoulders! All the way to My sacred mountain at Jerusalem! As of old when the children of Israel brought me a pure vessel and I chose from among them My priests and Levites.*

The sublime prophecies uttered by an inspired voice during the eighth century B.C. have for the most part been fulfilled. Not too long ago we witnessed in Rome the consecration of several bishops from Asia and Africa. How many miracles I have seen in my short span of eighty-three years! In my ears still ring the chuckles of cynics who poked fun at the work of missionaries and gravely doffed their hats to the colorful idols of the Far East. Where are the colorful idols today? By contrast, in China as well as in Vietnam, strong native Christian movements have developed. Half of Africa has been won over, and the news that I receive from Japan fills my aged heart with joy!

I might be criticized for ending this long statement with an outburst of enthusiasm, much like the Hebraic *selah* which explodes at the end of the psalms. For Christianity, forced to take refuge at the tip of the European peninsula, might be said to be threatened by the most frightful menace of all time. I have no fear. One should not be upset by the noise, the disorder, and the dust of a quarry. A quarry like the planet described by Termier in his account of the pounding and grinding sledge of the Dalmatian Alps. *Confractione confringetur terra*, says Isaiah.

Contritione conteretur terra, commotione commovebitur terra, sicut ebrius, et auferetur sicut tabernaculum unius diei. How beautiful is the sight of the whole earth, shaken to its very roots, moving toward the white figure who stands on the immovable rock with arms extended above the human multitudes and seems to be simultaneously beckoning, stopping, blessing and, like the conductor of an orchestra according to a psalm, tempering them! The legions of God, predicted by Ezekiel, ask nothing more of us than the very fate to which they are entitled. And under the pressure of these frightful forces, for the first time since the Roman Empire we see drawn up and organized, as the offspring of agreement and necessity, the figure of Europe. It is to be hoped that the unity of interests imposed by a common threat will be followed in a future less distant than we think, perhaps, by an attempt at spiritual unity. All of us—Catholic, Protestant and Jew—who believe in one God who is transcendent and good, and who was given to the men of all times through the Bible, should feel as brothers in the face of the nameless bestiality that has reared its head in the East. I give all good intentions and diplomatic efforts their due. But something has happened which is more important than all the Mechlin conferences and ecumenical palavers. It is that for more than thirty years all of us—Catholics, Protestants and Jews—have spilled blood for the same cause and in the same sacred name, the name of God. We have shared in a profuse communion of blood which it is not blasphemous to compare to the blood of Abel that reeks daily on our altars. And we should never forget that in this inordinate holocaust, our Biblical brothers of the Old Testament have borne more than their share of the most direct and demoniacal manifestation of the wrath of God. From every battlefield, crematory and concentration camp I hear a single inarticulate cry: "Father, let them be one, as we are one!"

CHAPTER II

The Old Testament Must Be Given Back to the Christian People

The Old Testament must be given back to the Christian people. Their pressing need for it outweighs all else. Christians must not be deprived of half of their heritage; they must not be driven from the Promised Land flowing with milk and honey. They must be given back for their own use their great edifice of the Bible, shorn of all the pseudoscientific apparatus of arbitrary conjectures and frivolous hypotheses that serve but to dishearten, to disconcert and to rebuff the faithful; to deafen them to such an extent that they, surrounded by the ridiculous clatter of scribes incapable of arriving at anything in the least articulate or positive, no longer hear the loud voice of the prophets. Sitientes, venite ad aquas! *In the magnificent work of the Holy Ghost, of the Wisdom of God, they must be shown, not a shapeless mass of unrelated materials half eaten away by time, but a superb monument untouched by the centuries and still available to us, intact and virginal, in its profound and sublime composition, in its original meaning and in the invitation—just as compelling today as it was then—that it extends to our intelligence, our imagination, our feelings and our needs for love and beauty. We are fortunate in having a transcription of the sacred text—a match-*

less transcription which has been sanctioned for centuries by the authority and practice of the Church—in which I see the masterpiece, the crowning and the glory of the Latin language: I have in mind the Vulgate.

If I had the final say, the Vulgate would form the basis for the education of children, just as Homer's poems, which it surpasses by far, once formed the basis for the education of young Greeks. Or if I had to settle for French translations, I would insist that they use this venerable canon as their guide and follow it closely; in it I seem to recognize the tone, the very accent of the Divinity. How fortunate we are in having recovered our heritage! In being able to marvel freely and openly at our God, our Creator, who appears even more plainly in the vivid word distinctly addressed to us than in the radiant confusion of nature! Let us feed on this story which has a meaning, this series of events presided over by God for our enlightenment and for the revelation of His infinite and ingenious mercies. No longer is God the cold entity of the philosophers. He is Somebody. Through Moses and David we see Him as He is, as He lives His life and as we who are made in His image have the right to see Him: let scholars explain that as they will . . .

But how joyous and moving to see our Father living up there and brimming over, it seems to us, with fatherly love, tenderness, compassion, and every other necessary feeling, including even anger! Yes, we love His holy anger; we like to be taken seriously in our transgressions as well as in our efforts to do good. And all the imbeciles who talk about an angry God! A jealous God, yes, as jealous as you please! That is the way we like it . . .

Let us plunge fearlessly, headfirst, into the ocean of love and beauty of the Old Testament, where so many Saints and spirits have found everlasting nourishment. Let us meet again, as they were in real life, truly superhuman people, people through whom the whole human race was completely trans-

figured by authentic signification: Abraham, Jacob, Joseph, Moses, Job, Samuel, David. They are not heroes drawn from novels or from the theatre. They are our brothers and sisters, but brothers and sisters flooded with Good; they are filled to overflowing with the Will of the Highest. Let us read the Holy Writ, but let us read it as did the Fathers who showed us the best way of profiting by it; let us read it kneeling! Let us read it, not critically with the foolish curiosity that leads only to vanity, but with the eagerness of a famished heart! We are told that life is there, that light is there. Why not make a slight effort to taste for ourselves? The Sinaitic Majesty is not the only one who invites us to the ascension! We are also invited by a feminine smile; it is the smile of Wisdom of the august Virgin whose image was set before the Lord to encourage Him to create the world! We can make out her figure at the end of the long line of matchless monuments. From the time of Genesis she was the progressive brightness that precedes the sunrise. For Christians the divine light of the Virgin is never absent from any part of the revealed text, either the Old Testament or the New. These words of the Savior, found in the Gospels, may apply to her: "Wherefore if they shall say unto you, Behold, He is in the desert, go not forth; He is in the secret chambers, believe it not. For as the lightening cometh out of the East and shineth even unto the West, so shall also the coming of the Son of man be." *He reigns throughout all parts of the Old Testament, which He inspired, as well as the New. He countersigned every page of both with this solemn oath:* "EGO VIVO!"

CHAPTER III

The Holy Scriptures

The Book of Kings tells us that David, having reached a ripe old age, tried to make up for his lack of vital heat by procuring a young girl, whose Hebraic name of Abishag is translated by some commentators as *Superabundance of the father* and by others as *Roaring,* to share his bed. And in my old age I too, as old or older in years than Christ's ancestor, met a virgin whose beauty surpasses by far the beauty of poor Abishag and whose youth cannot be compared with hers since it is the youth of eternity. I have in mind the Holy Scripture. In Scripture we find a *superabundance of the father,* and as for its *roaring,* which dominates every earthly sound, the lowliest pebble is enough to give voice to the vast sea itself. Scripture has the secret to the deep, vital burning that filled the hearts of Cleopas and his companion on the road to Emmaus while the Lord Himself, according to the Gospel of St. Luke, opened the holy text to them. And surely he joined to his explanations the sublime exhortation found in Chapter 4 of the Book of Proverbs:

"Get wisdom, get understanding: forget it not; neither decline from the words of my mouth. Forsake her not, and she shall preserve thee: love her, and she shall keep thee. Wisdom is the principal thing; therefore get wisdom: and

*with all thy getting get understanding. Exalt her, and she
shall promote thee: she shall bring thee to honour, when
thou dost embrace her. She shall give to thine head an orna-
ment of grace: a crown of glory shall she deliver to thee."*

The inebriation of the Scriptures, the strength of the mysterious wine which the Betrothed of the Song of Songs gives
her lover to drink—*come,* says she, *and drink abundantly, my
beloved*—is attested by the early Christians who, surfeited
with the bitter, unappetizing electuaries of pagan literature,
put the sacred cup to their lips. People fled into the desert to
do nothing day and night except to recite psalms. Huge
crowds crowded around Origen and his rivals whose homilies
are no more than a paraphrase of the lesson of Emmaus. For
fifteen centuries all thought, all art and all Christian literature
stemmed solely from intelligent and inspired meditation on
the inexhaustible Book. Later still, from a Bible discovered
at his uncle's house, Bossuet received the bolt from the blue,
the flash of sunlight that determined his vocation. There is
no point in mentioning Pascal and his mystical interpretations of the Scriptures, which adopt the spirit of the ancient
Fathers and which, in my opinion, form the most interesting
part of his *Thoughts.*

But my view is open to criticism. One objection is that the
Bible seems like a collection of unrelated documents. In it
are found examples of every known literary genre—history,
lyrical poems, philosophical treatises, novels, and even a
dramatic effort spanning half-mythical and early Christian
times. Yet I hold that the Bible typifies not merely one body,
but one person.

My answer is the conclusion forced on all serious students
of the prodigious work: the Bible, far from being a mass of
unrelated documents, is an edifice constructed of harmonious
materials; it is a living being that grows and develops before
our eyes, like the acorn that is destined from the outset to be
an oak and nothing else. Everywhere, behind different drag-

omen, different styles, different forms and different occasions, we find the same author with the same message. His rich resources are everywhere the same.

The author, as all faithful Catholics know, is the Holy Ghost. What a wonderful, transplendent privilege for us to have, within the confines of a book, the Holy Ghost which is said to be capable of *suggesting all things to us!* With what faith, with what respect, with what zeal we should consult it! We are not only advised, we are commanded to do so. *Search the Scriptures,* said the Savior. This does not mean a mere cursory glance, but earnest study requiring all our resources; I mean not only the scant resources of our minds and hearts but also the bountiful resources which are majestically unfolded by the doctrine and liturgy of the Church. *Ask now the beasts,* we are told in the Book of Job. Which beasts? Why, the Four Beasts that dominate the vast gospel consisting of the two Testaments with a single message: the Ox, the Lion, the Eagle and the Lamb.

But to say that we question the Scriptures is incorrect. It is better to admit that the Scriptures question us and find for each of us, throughout every age and generation, the right question. At the end of the extraordinary document called the Book of Job, we see the Eternal, as if nonplused by the vociferations of the prototype of Hus, take the floor, not to answer him but to question him. *I will demand of thee,* said He, *and answer thou Me.*

Where wast thou when I laid the foundations of the earth? Declare, if thou hast understanding. Who hath laid the measures thereof, if thou knowest? Or who hath stretched the line upon it? Whereupon are the foundations thereof fastened? Or who laid the corner stone thereof? When the morning stars sang together, and all the sons of God shouted for joy?

Are we being questioned by the Lord in such extraordinary terms? Is the Holy Ghost questioning us through the Scriptures? Or is He questioning something older than we—

something which was at the outset, at our beginning—and
something meant in the Gospel of St. John when the Lord
answered the question, *Who art thou?* by saying, *Even the
same that I said unto you from the beginning?* The Same that
speaks to you and is capable of speaking in you. The unknown
in us which is capable of giving the right answer only to the
right question. The unknown in us which is capable of "coming out" only at the bidding of its Creator. *Lazare, veni foras!*

That is what the Holy Scripture should be for all Christians
and that is the great good that they would draw from it if,
like their fathers, they continued to read it with pure hearts
and just intentions. But, alas, a terrible catastrophe has oc-
curred in the history of the Church. The rise of Protestant-
ism is as terrifying as the account of the Levite of Ephraim
found in the Book of Judges. A Levite who was returning
from Bethlehem was forced to expose his concubine to the
bestial rut of the citizens of Gabaa all night long. The next
morning, he found her at the doorsill, *sparsis manibus*. She
lay dead, her arms outstretched. No, the Scriptures are not
dead, but the Church in its wisdom and discretion has deemed
it necessary during the recent centuries not to expose them
to ignorant or perverse inquirers. The Church has been
obliged to devote itself almost exclusively to a mere apologetic
task, the pious charge of defending the abused body of the
Scriptures against predatory animals. Here a line from Virgil
comes to mind:

Obscoenique canes importunaeque volucres.

But to continue. The sacred text tells us that the Levite cut
the corpse of his wife into pieces, into twelve pieces which
he sent as a solemn summons to the twelve tribes of Israel.
These pieces are the different lessons, the particular devotions
which make up the limbs and organs of the beautiful primitive body and which are also invitations, addressed to us, to
restore its unity.

Let my right hand forget her cunning and my tongue cleave to the roof of my mouth, the psalmist will later say, *if I forget thee, O Jerusalem!*

What we need today are not extracts or fragments but the original document—the dismembered cadaver which we can ask, like the prophet Ezekiel, again to become a living person through the union of its joints. To become whole again, we need nothing less than the Word made whole again—the whole, unabridged Word converted into speech. I mean the Word as sound and signification or, in St. Paul's words, as a mission, an epistle and a general invitation addressed to our innermost being. Only then do we understand and take upon ourselves the burning insistence of Psalm 119. Throughout the one hundred and seventy-six verses of this great psalm, King David tirelessly and repeatedly asks God to flood his heart with understanding, to fill his eyes, his ears and all his senses with "commandments," precepts and Scripture; he asks for more than a fleeting taste on his tongue; he asks for substance, an exact means and an enlivening force.

Such should be, but obviously is not, the spiritual position of most Christians today. Their respect for Scripture is boundless, but they show their respect mainly by their remoteness. Few of them have ever read Scripture, and I am speaking of neither the Old Testament nor the New, but only of the Four Gospels. And among the rare champions who have chanced to glance at the Gospels, few indeed realize that, far from standing alone, this wonderful monument rests on a solid foundation and raises for all ages a transplendent crown of elucidations which is ruled over and brought to the fulness of perfection, from the height of the timeless region, by the supreme gem of the Apocalypse.

Ignorance of the Bible is more than an insult to God! It is an emotional and intellectual loss! It is a loss to what is today called culture! And what a great responsibility weighs down on those entrusted with the life-giving spring, the waters of Bethlehem whose taste and power defy comparison! How much knowledge, industry and labor they have expended in examining the most trivial grammatical or syntactical details of the sacred text! We have been spared no historical, geographical or archeological finding and no hypothesis relating to circumstances or dates. How scrupulously they have pandered to the whims of any bloated upstart who happened to draw support from the mortarboard of a doctor from Berlin or Chicago, with no other result than that of breeding disgust or, worse still, a scepticism which can not always be tolerated! On this point, people have confided to me heart-rending and horrifying secrets.

And still it is a tradition—consubstantial, if I may say so, with its actual message—that Scripture was not written to provide scientific information or to satisfy curiosities. The sole purpose of each detail of the divine work is to speak to us about God. Here rabbis and the Church Fathers use the same language. Listen to Rabbi Eleazar, the son of Simeon Bar Jochai:

Accursed be the spirit of whoever pretends that the narratives of Scripture have no signification aside from their literal meaning! For, if this were true, Scripture would not be the law of truth, holy law, and heavenly law. Even a king of flesh and bone would deem it beneath his dignity to say commonplace things and, to an even greater extent, to write them. Surely the supreme King, the Holy of Holies, could have found more sacred things to illustrate His law than simple tales like the story of Esau, Laban, the ass of Balaam, Balak and Zamri. It is not because of such stories that Scripture is called truth, perfect law, attested law, law more precious than gold and spices. But each word of Scripture conceals a mystery."[1]

[1] The text is taken from Zohar; apparently it is of recent date (13th century), but Paul Vulliaud, among other specialists, says that he made use of ancient documents. Rabbi Reb Aqiba expresses a similar belief.

And in the same way, following the footprints of St. Paul, Origen said in the second century A. D.:

If at times you come across a difficult passage while reading Scripture, blame only yourself and do not despair of finding out its true meaning. In this way you will bring to light what is written: Whoever believes will not be left in darkness.[2] Believe first and you will find a great and holy treasure hidden under the apparent offense. We are ordered not to utter an idle word lest we be held accountable on Judgment Day. This suggests that every word that drops from the prophets' lips has a purpose. I hold as certain that every written letter of the divine text[3] has its function and that every iota or accent of the Holy Writ has perceptible worth and power. The herbs of the fields have their individual properties with respect to bodily health or any other need, and yet not all people know what a particular herb is good for; the only ones who know its properties are those who can recognize the plant and are sufficiently versed in plant lore to know how to gather and prepare it, and where to place it on the body in order to benefit its user. Similarly, the holy, spiritual man knows how to select each iota or element of the Holy Writ; he knows the worth of each element and realizes that no part of Scripture is superfluous.

And then, on top of Origen, fifteen centuries of critical studies and patristic literature as well as all art, all thought, all liturgy and all prayers of the Catholic Church!

And now, unfortunately, from the height of Christian pulpits, authoritative voices accuse this vast, venerable and healthful effort of being *arbitrary,* as if arbitrariness were not the essence of most critical literature today: capriciousness and vanity are its trademark.

It is important to understand the meaning of the words "original text of the Scriptures" as used by the Council of

---

[2] Pascal, *Thoughts.*
[3] Cf. the *Tau* of Ezekiel and the *Alpha* and *Omega* of the Apocalypse.

Trent. The phrase applies to the Septuagint, which antedates the advent of the Savior by two centuries, not to the so-called Masoretic text of the *Codex Babylonicus Petropolitanus,* which dates from 1818 A. D.

On this point a Protestant, Mr. Arthur Samuel Deake, Professor of Biblical criticism at the University of Manchester, has this to say:

"All of our manuscripts represent one and the same text, the Masoretic. It was drawn up by a special team of qualified scholars whose aim was not only to preserve and transmit the available vowel-consonant text but also to indicate how to pronounce it correctly. To do so, they had to devise a whole system of vocalic points and accents.

. . . It is certain that, before the second century B.C. the different manuscripts of the Old Testament differed appreciably from each other; sufficient proof is provided by the Samaritan Pentateuch and translations, especially that of the Septuagint. Indications that the text was treated with considerable freedom in ancient times are not lacking in the Hebrew text itself.

. . . The old translations, especially that of the Septuagint, frequently show variations with respect to the Hebrew which not only are intrinsically more probable but which often explain the difficulties presented by the Masoretic text. Our estimation of the value of these variant readings is considerably heightened when we consider that the manuscripts on which the translations are based are several centuries older than those from which the Masoretic text was taken: the text which they presuppose thus has a fair claim to consideration as an important witness to the Hebrew original."

It should be noted that a number of Biblical citations made by St. Paul differ appreciably not only from the Masoretic text, but from the text of the Septuagint.

We are indeed fortunate to have such a translation of the Bible as the Vulgate. I personally, am almost willing to consider this poetic monument the masterpiece of the Latin language. If it is not inspired in the theological sense, it certainly is inspired in the literary sense, as when we say that the Iliad and the Aeneid are inspired works. There is, then, every reason to tremble on seeing men qualified only by erudition dare to meddle with it. After all, the test of bread is nourishment, the test of a remedy is healing, and the test of life is animation. The Vulgate has always proven itself to be, for saints and sinners alike, an inexhaustible source of instruction, enthusiasm, consolation and enlightenment. It is something like the Eucharist which is the root of paradise and the very language of our intercourse with God. In the absence of an original text, the Septuagint being the translation which is admittedly closest to it, it is hard to understand the authority peremptorily attributed to the single Masoretic text.

I feel that I am not exaggerating when I say that the unwarranted vogue of the Masoretic text derives for the most part from pedantic snobbery and from the timid, middleclass taste of most modern scholars. I am reminded of the druggist who is ashamed of the loud dress of his peasant grandmother. And then, good heavens! Above all, one must avoid hurting one's Protestant and pagan confreres!

Modern scholarship presents a sorry spectacle. Scholars everywhere are again taking up the work of St. John the Baptist; but they are taking it upon themselves, by dint of dishonest labor, to change harsh words into platitudes. The modern interpretation of the Scriptures reminds me of the quip of Jules Renard: "They have put so much water into their wine that there is no wine left."

Let the Vulgate be read, then, and let it be read in the right way, kneeling.

Then the mystical virgin, awakened by the kiss of grace in the first verse of the Song of Songs, in her constant search through the streets and crossroads of the city, will no longer have to ask the rude traffic wardens what they did with the

One whom her heart loves, and where they put Him after they carried Him away. She will find Him, lead Him into her mother's house, and share with Him a certain cup; He will in turn instruct her, teaching her who she is, for she does not know. And who knows whether, at the end, this happy creature will not hear herself invited by her guide to ascend with Him, still higher, the mountain of whiteness, the mountain of Lebanon. *Come!* we read in the Song, *Come, my spouse. Come, thou shalt be crowned.* What crown does he mean? Not a narrow circle, though it were golden, cut to the measure of our temples, but one encompassing the vast horizon surrounding us and reaching as high as we can climb; he means the catholic horizon consisting of all of heaven and earth in their fulness!

NOTE

The directors of *Vie intellectuelle*, the periodical in which the preceding article appeared, inserted on the following pages, doubtlessly as an antidote, an *Apology for Literalism*, signed by Father Jean Steinmann. As an eminent exponent of the most radical trend in Biblical criticism, Father Steinmann minimizes *allegorism*. Always conscious of the pallid, or let us say cadaveric, appearance of texts studied under the light of literalism, the ecclesiastic invites his readers to practice *intuition*. This means, he says, "putting one's self into the skin" of the deceased authors whose lives were pre-empted or, putting it another way, substituting a product of the imagination for their souls.

The task is not easy. For who were the deceased authors? Literalist critics have taken pains to cleanse them of any secular taint. After the professors have completed their work, the remains look less like human beings than anatomical compositions consisting of parts that were cleanly dismembered and awkwardly reassembled in defiance of vital functions. For example, what are we to do with the mangled Isaiah shown to us, a smile on his lips, by Jack the Ripper?

Missing from the creations of modernist butchery is the life which the Holy Ghost communicated to Christ's two witnesses before they were publicly displayed in the square of the great town known spiritually as "Egypt and Sodom." St. Paul tells us in II Timothy that *all scripture is given by inspiration of God, and is profitable for doctrine, for reproof, for correction, for instruction in righteousness.* Father Steinmann would have us believe that inspiration was withheld from St. Jerome, yet guided his prosecutors' knives.

CHAPTER IV

The Meaning of the Holy Scriptures

Paris, March 11, 1949.

Dear Reverend Father,

I read Father J. Steinmann's article in the current issue of *Vie Intellectuelle* very carefully. Under the pretext of an imaginary conversation between Pascal and the Oratorian Richard Simon, the author ambiguously sets forth his ideas on the literal and figurative meaning of the Scriptures.

The subject is of such importance and touches on basic questions of such great interest to a Catholic heart and mind that it should have been dealt with fully and openly, on grounds cleared of circumlocutions.

In the imaginary dialogue, it is apparent that the author is in full sympathy with the daring seventeenth-century exegete who was so severely and, in my opinion, so unjustly reprimanded by Bossuet.

I pass over the doubts expressed by Mr. Stienmann concerning the textual authenticity of the sacred Books. "Will you deny," he asks through his spokesman, "that the text, once it had been set down by the pen of inspired scribes, was

43

transmitted to us by generations of copyists each of whom was as liable to error *as you and I?*" He tells us to ferret out the mistakes and correct them, as if uninspired authors were to blame for them.

Mr. Steinmann says nothing of the Church, which nevertheless has something to say on the subject.

He seems not to be aware of the great danger of introducing free and individual criticism to the study of texts which the Church has given us to read as the authentic word of God. Doubt is not given its due.

But these remarks make up only a preamble: the poignant interest that forced me to take pen in hand lies elsewhere. To a Christian, touching the Scriptures is like touching the Eucharist.

Mr. Steinmann, through his spokesman, contradicts Pascal —who joined with all the Fathers and with the Traveler of Emmaus Himself in affirming that the presence of Jesus Christ was announced, proclaimed and anticipated from the beginning to the end of the Old Testament—by saying that Christ *brought to the texts a richness that they lacked.* What does he mean? Are we to understand that he rules out any Messianic intention?

Surely Mr. Steinmann does not think that the editors of the Old Testament had no idea of the great events of which God made them heralds, the Incarnation and the Redemption. Or that the New Testament came to rest on the substructure of the Old, whose editors foresaw nothing of the future, through some special arrangement of Providence.

What of texts like *Abraham vidit et gavisus est* (*John* 8:56)? What of the prophecy of Isaiah? What of the continuous interventions of God, directly or through His Angels, from the beginning of the Bible to the end? And so on.

What of the proclamation of the Church which joins St. Paul in affirming that not just some, but *all* parts of scripture are divinely inspired? What of the Credo that we recite aloud every Sunday? Does he think that the prophets are like the Ass of Balaam in that the true meaning of their words is elusive? In short, are they people who do not know what they are saying?

When God told David to *sit at His right hand,* was this order meant solely and exclusively for the Holy King?

Mr. Steinmann serenely maintains that the Old Testament has but one meaning, the literal meaning, and this of course is the basest and most vulgar meaning possible. What does he think of the vast body of patristic literature which has inspired so much beauty and devotion and which, for more centuries than I can count, has held the opposite view? Is he trying to refute this whole august tradition? Not only the Church Fathers, but also the Pope speaking through his encyclical letter *Providentissimus* and the whole of Catholic liturgy?

Mr. Steinmann shows an amusing condescension for the early clients who, according to him, had exclusive rights to the most profound and sublime documents that have ever honored Mankind. Shall we dare to ask him whether in his opinion revelation was addressed to those clients alone, or whether the message of Moses and the prophets continues still today to concern all countries and all ages?

I should be very grateful to you if it were possible for you to publish my letter in the next issue of *Vie Intellectuelle.*[1]

Sincerely yours,

PAUL CLAUDEL

P.S.—Mr. Steinmann tells us that the "inventor of figurative interpretation" was Origen. I had always believed that it was St. Paul.

[1] Publication was refused.

May 3, 1949.

Dear Reverend Father,

I have studied Steinmann's[2] letter, which you were so kind as to communicate to me, and wish to make the following comments on the subject:

(1) Father Steinmann pretends that, in the conversation which he imagines, his thought is expressed by neither Richard Simon (a quasi-heretic) nor Pascal (a heretic) but by Mr. de Sacy (another heretic). De Sacy fails to contradict Richard Simon's strange theses relating to Faith. He has recourse to "Charity." "Scripture is," he says, "the realm of the heart and feelings where beauty is grasped intuitively . . . we leave the rational realm of criticism . . . and enter the domain of prayer. The Bible, from the first word of Genesis to the last word of the Apocalypse, was written to reveal divine charity. To speak to us, the Scriptures had to become a child along with us children and stammer to avoid dazzling us."

Until this day I had always thought that Scripture was not limited to feelings but that it dealt with exact predictions concerning the Savior and the circumstances of His mission, in accordance with the text of St. John: *Scripturae sunt quae testimonium perhibent de Me* (*John* 5:39).

(2) Father Steinmann is perfectly willing to admit in the letter addressed to you that such prophecies exist, but he draws a line between texts that are "obviously Messianic" and texts that are not. I should like to know his criterion for making the distinction.

(3) But Father Steinmann's Richard Simon goes much further, even to the point of denying a spiritual meaning. This is what he writes: "The Bible consists of texts, and the texts *have but one meaning*, the primary literal meaning, the one intended by the holy writer." It seems he is treading on thin ice when he makes this categorical statement.

[2] Publication of Father Steinmann's reply was refused.

(4) Father Steinmann seems to hold to his statement that "the inventor of figurative interpretation" was Origen. Others speak of St. Paul and of the Savior Himself.

(5) On the basis of what evidence does Father Steinmann maintain that "Pascal and Mr. Claudel state that the *only* true meaning of the Old Testament is the spiritual meaning?" I clearly said the opposite and affirmed my respect for the literal meaning, which is not always the only meaning. Neither Pascal nor I has ever pretended that "the literal meaning is the basest and most vulgar meaning possible." This statement, which in no way concerns Pascal, applies on my part, not to the literal meaning proper but to the way it is interpreted by a great number of modern Protestant and —alas!—Catholic exegetes. Proofs and illustrations are not hard to find. One has only to open the Crampon Bible, which is unfortunately the only Bible in the hands of the public today.

(6) Father Steinmann cites freely the Encyclical *Divino afflante spiritu.* I bow respectfully before the authority of His Holiness. Still, his authority should not be abused. The sort of textual and grammatical expurgation which he obviously has in mind should not be cited to prove that he sanctions complete freedom of individual interpretation in modern or modernistic criticism. I intend to give below some of the abuses that such freedom leads to.

(7) I should like to know what gives Father Gélin, translator of the prophet Zechariah in the most recent revision of the Bible, the right to substitute the word "body" for the word "hands"—and that without any explanatory note to readers—in a text which many outmoded minds still consider Messianic (*Zechariah* 13:6).

—I should like to know whether the Encyclical in question authorizes P. Dubarle in his book on the *Sages d'Israël* (*Éditions du Cerf,* p. 15) to express himself as follows on one of the most fundamental texts of the Scriptures: "That is

why older versions, clarifying dubious suggestions of Genesis
with the hindsight of later interventions of divine Grace, saw
in this passage a positive announcement of the total defeat of
the tempter by an individual savior, and even a woman's
participation in his triumph: a justifiable overstatement, but
still an overstatement of the original text."

—In one passage Father Steinmann recounts in his own way
the notion that he thinks Pascal would have of the figurative
role of the personages of the Old Testament: "Jesus Christ
the Father in Abraham, Jesus Christ the lawgiver in Moses,
and Jesus Christ the King in David." Mr. Steinmann adds:
"Yes, but on condition that you are fully aware that you are
thereby bringing to the texts of the Old Testament *a richness that they lacked.*" In plain English: "You are making a
mistake." And yet Our Lord tells us that it is "in spirit" that
David prophetically called Him *Lord and Son* (*Matthew*
22:43).

(8) Father Steinmann reminds me that the Encyclical
Divino reduced the spiritual meaning strictly to what is
taught on the subject in the New Testament. Certainly, but
this authorization is far-reaching. For this is what we read in
the Gospel of St. Matthew: *For verily I say unto you, Till
heaven and earth pass, one jot or one tittle shall in no wise
pass from the law, till all be fulfilled* (*Matthew* 5:18). Thus
He affirms and guarantees the spiritual value of the Law of
Moses *in every detail.* Father Steinmann, answering Pascal
through the mouth of his dragoman, says: "The rites of the
Old Testament are symbolic, you tell me, and you see in
them images of Jesus Christ. You have left the realm of the
Bible proper. For the Bible consists of texts, and the texts
continue to have but one meaning, the primary, literal meaning, the one intended by the holy writer."

But there in another text of the New Testament—St. Paul
is after all a part of the New Testament—of still wider scope.
This sweeping text is the famous verse of I Corinthians

10:11: *Haec omnia contingebant illis in figura.* Yes, Father, it is clearly written: *omnia,* and it is also clearly written *in figura: typicôs, typice,* and also *omnia.*

—A final example. Now, following Mr. Dubarle (*op. cit.,* p. 79), Father Steinmann attacks a formidable text which the Church has made a part of its liturgy and which has given comfort and consolation to I know not how many souls: "*I know that my redeemer liveth, etc.*" (*Job* 19:25–27). Through an erroneous translation, says Father Steinmann, misleading notions about resurrection are attributed to Job. Almost all the Church Fathers have seen in Job's words an unmistakable profession of faith in the resurrection of the body; during the first centuries of the Church, pious Christians had this act of faith engraved on their tombs as an expression of their own beliefs. St. Jerome admirably sums up the traditional interpretation in these luminous lines: *Resurrectionem corporum sic prophetat, ut nullus de ea vel manifestius vel cautius scripserit* (*Epistles* 53:8). As a plain, ignorant believer, I ask: Should we believe the Church, St. Jerome and the Church Fathers? Or should we believe men like Father Steinmann and P. Dubarle who openly and scathingly contradict them? Do they really think that they have the right to invoke the Encyclical *Divino affleante spiritu* to justify their attitude?

In my ears still ring the vituperative words of August Rodin, addressed to the "restorers" of his time who destroyed priceless monuments of classical art and replaced them with individual creations in the style of Louis Philippe and Napoleon III. Here we are not concerned with glass or passive stone but with living texts that contain the actual word of God! Will no authoritative voice rise up in protest against the unbridled and tasteless boldness of exegetical Viollet-le-Ducs?

The fact is that two conflicting concepts determine how

the Old Testament, and consequently the New, should be interpreted.

According to the first, the Bible is a human work into which are inserted—no one knows exactly how, but somewhat like raisins into a plum cake—Messianic texts which critics would diminish as much as possible in number and importance. According to the second, the Bible is a divine work inspired by the Holy Ghost, which thoroughly penetrates every part of it, and its meaning is Jesus Christ, our Redeemer, truly the son of God and truly the son of man.

Depending on the concept adopted, textual criticism is conducted along wholly different lines and leads to wholly different results.

I note with regret and—why not say so?—indignation, that not the second but the first of these concepts is apparently the one generally accepted today.

Sincerely yours,

PAUL CLAUDEL

CHAPTER V

The Prophetic Spirit

There are two ways of looking at an event, depending on whether its source or its result is under consideration. To generalize, one attitude is characteristic of the scholar, the other of the poet. One relates to causes; the other relates to the effect and sees only a concatenation of means in the causes. One describes how forces act on matter in the most painstaking detail possible; the other starts from results and looks intelligently and sympathetically on the whole network of routes which have converged there from all directions for a single purpose. From the second point of view, every freedom called into service by the world had but one aim.

But the first mental set has prevailed for several centuries. Under the influence of Descartes, we have clung to a mechanistic concept of the universe. The relations between facts are expressed mathematically: a given set of facts will invariably produce a predictable effect. This view is attractive by virtue of the satisfaction that it offers a mind eager for exactness; it also holds great practical interest since it endows us with an instrument of almost unlimited power.

It is more important to conquer the world than to understand it, according to this view; we should learn about the world in order to exploit it; we should subordinate all knowl-

edge to utility, and rid our minds of why in order to inquire
into how. The effective cause among scholars is invested with
exclusive authority, and the final cause, far from being merely
discredited, is anathema.

The best illustration of the first view is afforded by
Marxist theory. Here manual labor is the predominant
source of value; all profit goes to the worker; no previous
deduction is sanctioned. But value obviously had a completely different origin, and that is the consumer's demand
for the manufactured item. An eccentric might spend years
in inscribing the Civil Code on a peach stone without adding
anything at all to the value of the stone. Against this, a glass
of water acquires incalculable worth in the desert. The laborer's work in the production of an item is but one element,
and often the least important element, in fixing its final
worth. His salary is thus a lawful payment for a limited contribution and not a ransom paid for a basic injustice. Value
depends on the final cause, which is the demand and taste of
the consumer, and not on the effective cause, which is the
worker—and certainly not on the worker alone!

In literature, the predominance of the effective cause inspired the theory of art for art's sake. What the writer has to
say is unimportant; the important thing is how he says it. All
the theoretical writing of Paul Valery is devoted to promot-
ing this absurdity; fortunately, the work of the master poet
contradicts his theory. Soon we shall come back to this subject.

I realize that today this statement, though drawn from a
common-sense observation, seems somewhat scandalous: in
the beginning is the end.

In the beginning was demand. The world was made on demand. A demand which God's right hand passed to His left
hand. A demand which the Power of the Creator directed to
the power (in the scholastic sense) of His creature. A demand which the requirements of one directed to the freedom

of the other. A healthy economy, by contrast with Marxist theories, is known to put the product ahead of the process, or to put more stress on the final cause and less on the effective cause. A Marxist economy exploits the known; a healthy economy appeals to the unknown, to progress and to inventiveness. Take a problem of military procurement—say a plane or a tank. According to Marxist theory, a closely regimented bureau sends detailed plans, drawn up on the basis of controlled experiments, to the factory. The plans submitted must be followed to the letter. In a free economy, on the contrary, a client submits to competitors a proposal for an item that meets with certain specifications as to its speed, armament, safety features, price, etc.—a list of contractual conditions, I believe it is called. The supplier has the task of deciphering them and subsequently of calling into action, from the top to the bottom of the hierarchical ladder, a whole line of collaborators and sub-contractors, from the engineer to the last laborer. The supplier runs the gamut of possibilities in recruiting both technical skills and raw materials in order to achieve a superior and financially satisfactory result. This gives unlimited range to individual initiative. In the same way Napoleon, by contrast to the rigid tactical notions of the preceding century, scheduled meetings with collaborators at various points on the map in order to bring about the capitulation of his opponent. Intelligence, imagination, and will took first place and determined the means. Or take Homer: the muse proposed and imposed as subjects the wrath of Achilles and the return of Ulysses. His assignment was not laboriously to discharge a task or to color in haphazardly a design outlined beforehand. His assignment was rather an event which was insignificant in itself but which—like all other events—when viewed with intensity and depth, called the whole roster of men and gods into action and left unemployed none of the emotions or *powers* of our nature. The prosodic material itself was chosen to serve not merely as a vehicle, but as a source of inspiration.

God is not envious of His work. All that He created, He created in emulation of His own excellence. Intolerant of inertia, He provoked movement, and then, into movement, He introduced the principle of movement which is life. For He is the supreme Living One. When Moses questioned Him, He replied that His name was: I AM. But when the time of eruption came, the moment that marked the end of His putting Himself into the mouths of His prophets, then He revealed Himself by another name: I LIVE! *I live! Ego vivo! I have long time holden my peace; I have been still, and refrained myself: now will I cry like a travailing woman!* I am not merely a presence, I am an interpellation. And what would Christ say to those who asked for an accounting of His mission? *I am come that they might have life and that they might have it more abundantly. For I am the Way, the Truth and the Life.*

The Way is every means made available for our use; the Truth is the End envisioned; the Life is the body quickened within us by knowledge and the energy to answer the call directed to us. The same notion was expressed in a different sequence by St. Paul: *in God we live and move and have our being.* First he put life, which we have through conception; then the power of independent action; and finally, our ordination or emergence through affirmation as thinking persons with faces and names.

A person. Someone who says: I. Someone who needs another person and who, with each heaving of his chest, again asks the outer element for the power to be himself. Constantly he seeks some sort of revival or rekindling of himself. In God there is respiration; we worship a living God who works and breathes; our God breathes in His own Being. From St. Paul we learn that He is the One who gives *inspiration* to His image in every living being. And before St. Paul,

Job: *In whose hand is the soul of every living thing, and the breath of all mankind* (12:10). *He giveth breath unto the people upon it, and spirit to them that walk therein* (*Isaiah* 42:5). *Behold, all souls are mine* (*Ezekiel* 18:4). But I should never finish citing the texts that come to mind, starting from the most important one, the verse in the Book of Genesis (2:7) that shows us the Creator blowing the breath of life deep inside His creature—breath which He was to reclaim. The Word secretes in our hearts the speech that is shaped by our lips.

Everywhere Creation shows how initiative belonged to the final cause, which was the need which the Creator deemed it good to have of *that. His left hand is under my head,* says the Song of Songs, *and His right hand doth embrace me.* God's right was used to call into existence, co-existence and a state of awareness of Him, what His left hand prepared for Him through the agency of His Angels. *Let me see thy countenance, let me hear thy voice; for sweet is thy voice, and thy countenance is comely* (*Song of Songs* 2:14): the roaring of the lion as well as the cooing of the dove and the bleating of the lamb, not to mention the mewling of newborn infants.

And now, listen carefully! A variable Providence does not dispense nourishment *in an acceptable time,* as the psalm puts it, to show God's great love for His creature. Nor does God show His love by meting out exceptional natural or supernatural gifts to a chosen few. He shows His great love by allowing us to do something for Him. When St. Paul was blinded and struck down on the road to Damascus, his first words, strange as it may seem, were not words of thanks. They were: *Lord, what wilt thou have me to do?* And similarly, the first words of God's creature, from the lowliest depth to the loftiest height, are: Lord, what shall I do with the means that you have provided for my existence?

The idea of mere mechanical Evolution, as conceived un-

der the sign of the effective cause[1] during the last century, is
now dying out. It has come up against irrefutable objections.
Descartes, to whom the idea owes its origin, said that he, if
given space and movement—only that and nothing more!—
could reconstruct the world. The few amateurish attempts
that he made in this direction are not convincing. But
Descartes' conception of the world has been discarded today:
we need more than neutral, inert matter and an outside
stimulus to interpret the initial fillip ably and obediently.
Today we know that everything, including even mass (as
Leibnitz had suspected), can be reduced to movement or,
more specifically to energy. And energy, from the lowest to
the highest realms of physics and of life, can not exist apart
from its two governing constituents, direction and form. An
independent, self-contained unit, such as the Epicurean
atom, is nothing more than an abstraction. Everything exists
through its relation to something else and as a function,
planmaessig, of something else. We know that the scholastic
adage says that *acting follows being, agere sequitur esse;* we
also know that the reverse is true, that *being follows action.*
In examining a witness, we must first find out what *he does*
and what *he is doing here,* as if he were a character in a play.
We must learn what he does with the particle of energy de-
posited in him and how he is outfitted and equipped. The
mechanistic notion still persists; at its crux is not however
the passive obedience of blind elements but rather an awareness of and a responsibility to varying degrees of lucidity,

[1] The end result of the effective Cause, of mechanism, of the least ruling
the most or of progress being constrained always to outdo itself, as Hegel
and Renan hold, is God! To them, the world is no longer the work of God;
God is rather the work of a world, condemned by I know not whom to the
forced labor of producing Him. "A fact is an arbitrary section: the law alone
exists, and everything is reduced to it." "Nature and history are but the
unfolding of universal necessity: the world forms a unique, indivisible being;
all beings are parts of it." "It is engaged in an undertaking which will have
as its final outcome (why final?) the full advent of God." (Ernest Renan,
cited by Jacques Chevalier in his book on Bergson, pages 8 and 9). In short,
he has to accept the final Cause, but only as the product of a blind effort.

initiative and talent that penetrates the whole crew, from the star player down to the electrician and prompter. A recruiting of wills in the service of the Order of the Day.

In the service. . . . But his name is none other than the Devil, the denizen of the void, who proudly proclaimed that *he would not serve,* and that he would serve no purpose (how wrong he was!). The last words of the One whom Isaiah called *my righteous Servant* (53:11) were pronounced before He surrendered to those who were seeking Him. His words were: *the Son of man came out to be ministered unto, but to minister.* We know that every living being (and who knows how far down the roots of life reach?) and every syllable uttered by the Word need to be served for the sole purpose of being enabled to serve more and to realize more fully the testimony which God entrusted to them and which gives them a purpose. That is why, as seen in Genesis, God called into existence ascending orders of creatures to serve each other and to procure their means of existence from each other; when man appeared he was told that he might *have dominion over* all of them and be served by each of them without serving any of them. But this did not free him from the holy law of service. Certainly not. Just as other creatures need each other for a temporal purpose, God needs man for a redemptive purpose. And to this end He gave man the Ten Commandments. The first of these requires man to serve Him, and be of service to Him, by denying him the right to go after something which does not exist. And by not preventing other men from serving Him and being of service to Him by harming their persons or their possessions.

St. Paul tells us that *the whole creation travaileth in pain* (*Romans* 8:22). St. John tells us why the whole creation labors: for the birth of the Son of God.[1] Creation had to give

---

[1] *But as many as received him, to them gave he power to become the sons of God* (1:12).

birth to man before man could give birth to the son of man. An inspired creation was the response to the Creator's *fiat* proposing birds and fishes, and *the holy child Jesus* was the inspired Virgin's response to His *fiat* proposing a son. This climaxed all the successive *fiats* through which Creation made use of its initial submission to God and rendered Him still greater service in accordance with his plan. God's plan was carried out through successive stages, not by virtue of an arbitrary decision, but in such a way that each "day" carried its contribution over to the next "day" and each "evening" is the dawn of a new "morning." First He created light, as if to see clearly, then the firmament embodying structural tenacity and distinctiveness. And then into matter consisting solely of movement held captive by form, He inserted something new: life. Here was an independent source of initiation, direction and modulation. From one "day" to the next there was no interruption or break, no alien contribution. Without light and space, there could have been no plant life. God "ordered" plant life as one would order furnishings for an existing workshop. It could also be said that He "asked" for it and that the whole arrangement, vaguely aware of its inherent *morning,* adapted itself *multifariam multisque modis* to the demands made upon it and fulfilled its secret pledge. The same thing happened when the Creator ordered or asked the land, water and air to produce—reptiles, fishes, birds, all other animals, and finally man of whom Ezekiel says *thy father was an Amorite, and thy mother an Hittite.*

The Book of Genesis gives us an indication of the casting by listing the broad classes of actors but tells us nothing about the actual drama. It does not tell us what the actors do individually and collectively, what challenges they faced, what their actions mean, or what tasks they are to carry to a successful conclusion. Not one could have existed all alone, without a cause—without all sorts of causes—behind him, without needs before him, and without all sorts of obligations beside

him. I leave out physico-chemical requirements, however ingenious or complicated their interpretation may be, and deal
only with that indispensable something shared by the actors,
the vital appetence which binds them to each other and
which we have every reason to call love.

First there is the difference between sexes through which
a new life issues from a mutual contribution. Unless it feeds
on plants, each living being must also seek nourishment from
other living beings, thus symbolizing the Communion of
Saints. Some animal communities are organized and ad-
ministered by a collective soul. There is the first rudiment of
prophetic inspiration, to be dealt with shortly, in the mysterious phenomenon of instinct and orientation. Take the insect
which performs an exacting surgical operation on another
unseen insect. Or the innate sense of direction shared by
many animal species and exemplified by the homing pigeon.
Or the migratory shuttling of birds. Or the eel: in him is the
vision of the nuptial abyss in the deepest part of the ocean
where death awaits him; nothing can prevent the young eel
from following the route that leads to the secluded nook for-
saken by his mother.

Up to this point we have not had an all-encompassing view
of the setting. We have limited ourselves to considering each
element in the light of its contribution to the setting. But the
Book of Ecclesiasticus, without contradicting the Book of
Genesis, tells us that God created all things at the same time.
The world is not a random heap of unrelated entities but a
living, coherent whole; the smooth functioning of its harmonious structure implies rhythmic action throughout all its
parts. Progressive specialization marks the arrangement of
the basic, common qualities of weight, movement, expanse,
atmosphere, light, temperature, electricity, physical and
chemical components, and the like; then some qualities are
characteristic of each kingdom and of each animal and vegetable species; such specialization extends to the particular

and to the individual. Still evident here, however, is the
schematic unity—I should prefer to say the programmatic
unity—indispensable to the play. That is why God's Creation
says in the Song of Songs: *His banner over me was love* (2:4).
This means that all beings can commune with each other and
do good to each other; they can render mutual help as they
work toward a common goal. The words must be interpreted
broadly to apply not only to material good and physical help
but also to the knowledge—the semantic contribution—
which each brings to every congener of his acquaintance.
Thus an isolated noun has but limited worth. But let an inspired writer add an illuminating adjective, use the noun to
prime and strengthen a moving sentence, and wring from it,
through other words, unity and action. Love is then boundless. Everything in this world can make everything else more
meaningful. We are in the bountiful realm of analogy, which
St. Bonaventure stated as a formula: *a is to b as c is to d.*
This formula is as fruitful for the scholar as it is for the
artist. It has been said that comparison and reasoning are not
the same, but reasoning would have no basis if comparison
had not first lighted and explored the infinite field of experience. I shall have more to say about this later.

Imagine an observer or, as they said in the eighteenth
century, a spy. Or perhaps even a critic like the one in charge
of the theatrical page of a Parisian newspaper. Suppose that
the intelligentsia of the planet Mars have commissioned him
to report to the intelligentsia of the planet Venus on the
strange intermediary particle which has been offending their
respective eyeballs for a long time. He lands from one of the
flying saucers which some Americans use to poke fun at the
credulity of others. He traverses our globe in every direction,
pries into all its secrets, and prepares to draw up his report.
"I shall not deal," he says, "with the cute traffic system (he
must have borrowed the word *cute* from some disreputable
associate) which is the life and breath of our neighbor Gaea.

That is the task of my scientific colleague. Hampered by my ignorance of their language, I shall speak only in generalities and include only the things that strike a philosopher's eye. I shall summarize my point of view by saying that Gaea impresses me first and foremost, in the elliptical course tirelessly and tenaciously followed through our cosmographical scheme, as offering a spectacular performance. Around the middle there is a fixed or stagnant zone where the climate does not change (compare it, if you will, to the wings); it is set aside for contemplation or for intensified maceration in the form of dreaming; when maceration gives way to despair, a frenzied revolt ensues. Then, to the north and to the south, a balanced repertory of regular performances. I am sure that the production is interesting, at least insofar as a casual tourist could delve into its meaning. I offer two facts as proof. First, the almost religious importance that nature seems to give to each of its actors or characters, the care that she exercises in preparing, arming, making-up, and "producing" them in every sense of the word; the unimaginable delicacy, patience and complexity of means which she uses; and the unrelenting harshness which she displays in subordinating the individual to the group—with the result that the unbridled multiplication of edible resources has as its counterpart the insatiable gullets of the devourers. Second, the drama—it would be more appropriate to call it the "parade" —is always the same. Renewed and repeated with indefinite variations of detail, the never-ending sequence of the seasons is always the same. The performance might be said to be designed to end for the sole purpose of beginning again. The necessity exists, and the performance must be *executed* at all costs. This suggests an invalid who has something very important to say but can not manage to make himself understood. His only resource is tirelessly to repeat himself, to keep repeating himself, over and over! And then, the stammerings having been duly noted, the conspicuous reappearance of the same leaves on the barren branches of the same tree in the spring-time. The same unpublished rose. And in some cranny of the snow-covered forest of fir-trees, the exact duplicate, complete in every detail, of the same dogtooth violet. 'But perhaps I shall manage to make myself understood by dint of repetition! In passing I have taken it upon myself to report on things which do not pass away.' "

And so his pen speeds over the paper and leaves behind an unchangeable *meaning*.

Science has multiplied our observations and references with respect to the scheme of space but has unfortunately left a void in our scheme of time. The void contains only a muddle of partial remains. But we should still appreciate one fact: the vast world that surrounds us does not exist but continues to exist; it is not there but rather continues to be there. To study it and understand it is not enough; we must listen to it and hear it out. To take in its notes is not enough; we must draw out its melodic line. We have just seen the conclusions drawn by our Saucerman concerning the importance which nature attached to her "Creations" (as we say of a *creation* of a dressmaker or music hall), and of the stress which she placed on repetition. Equally remarkable is her persistence, which is uninterrupted but amenable to modulation. Mountains are petrified modulations; they bear witness of the architectonic will which they obeyed with a violence that went as far as convulsion. But persistence marks the plain, too—and I say nothing about evaporation which would invite further thought—for there is something divine in the slope which the plain readies as an outlet, in the attentiveness and soft sound of the plain, and in the bristling of numberless and diverse senses through which vegetation immerses the plain at a certain moment and temperature. There is attentiveness to time. There is a perpetual and widespread conspiracy that spans the alternating periods which are constantly revived as if by respiration; something is going on; preparations are being made; by means of the verb, diverse complements are consorting with the predicate. There is imperceptible but genuine continuity.

In nature's continuous pattern, the crown passes from a lower to a higher kingdom: from the mineral kingdom to the vegetable, then to the animal, and finally to the human kingdom. This might be called *progress*, a word familiar to Christians today (December 8, 1952), for the worshiper is today shown the Almighty deliberating with the Church before creating the world, and the Church advancing through the ages and across nations *as the light of the morning when the sun riseth*. In the history of Mankind, the Scriptural emanation shows us—but how vaguely!—that there was first a period of dispersion and populating, of searching out new horizons; then came a period of condensation, consolidation and the development of a collective conscience.

For many centuries, and still today in Asia, human collectivities, like animal colonies, followed no pursuits other than those that enabled them to subsist on their own resources. Nothing more monotonous than a succession of identical dynasties—in China, for instance, and perhaps also in Egypt and Chaldea—succumbing in turn to the indifferent rhythm of their dawn, apogee, decline and fall. There were of course some external disturbances of a meteorological nature. Like passing tornadoes, they left behind a path of destruction; soon the intrusion was absorbed, however; balance was restored, leaving only wrinkles, and life surged on. In India, though an alien element in the form of Islam took root, an iron law that gripped every phase of society ruled out not only the possibility of change but even the desire for it and the notion of it. Unless the alternative of decay set in, the principle of sluggishness, contraction and stagnation turned up again in Islam, in the talmudic Judaism that replaced the old faith, and in the Orthodox Church—unleavened dough that will never rise again.

And now . . . I am searching for the right words . . . I
ask readers who do not share my beliefs to grant me the in-
dulgence which they would extend to a Moslem or Hindu
. . . I have mentioned the three natural kingdoms upon
which the human kingdom was superimposed: may I apply
the name of divine kingdom to the organic spark of restless-
ness, desire and discontent planted deep within the entrails
of Mankind? Unless I am wrong, scholars admit that the
forces of life work against the law of entropy or loss that
governs matter. It seems as if the acorn knows its destiny and
carries within itself an active idea of the oak required of it.
And in the same way it seems as if memory and foresight
join together in the hearts of Adam's sons to deny the immediate the right to prevail. We see them setting up doll-like
idols at fixed distances from pegs in order to stimulate, from
without, a certain taste for initiative and resistance. And I
have no right to neglect a stifled but tenacious tradition of a
primordial Creator repeatedly uncovered by Dr. Schmidt
among what are apparently the most degraded representa-
tives of the human race.

Man had not yet left the chaotic stage of mythical and
metaphysical reveries. Vague dreams were still to be replaced by intellectual attainments and strong wills. The order to *Rise up and walk!* had not yet been trumpeted. Mankind, blear-eyed and hamstrung, had not yet learned to use
the mainspring that would enable him to walk.

I have my own idea, but I should like here to assume the
point of view of a contractor. Obviously for the contractor,
who must make use of man's most distinctive traits and of
those qualities that set him furthest apart from animals,
danger lies in the immediate; the contractor will have to
brace him against the immediate. To a limited extent nature
herself teaches the animals to sacrifice the present to the future for the preservation and propagation of the species. The
family, clan and fatherland use co-operation to teach the in-

dividual the same lesson. But all these are not enough to reach down to the very roots of our being and enlist our full strength. Their pull, as we say, is not strong enough. They leave vast resources untapped. Man was made to serve and to serve a purpose with his whole being. *Ambula coram Me,* said God to Abraham, *et esto perfectus.* And man is not fully satisfied until the final cause in him is wholly and freely subordinated to effective causes. *Walk before Me,* and indeed, it is by walking before Him or according to His will that man achieves self-realization and perfection.

At last Mankind had begun to walk before God. After he had started to walk before Him, man realized for the first time that he was leaving behind an unbroken and decisive furrow[3] and sowing ever-widening commotion that would eventually engulf the whole planet. The result was that forever after, nothing happened except "before God;" the whole Story of Mankind was impregnated with meaning; it followed a straight course through events and became the Story of Christ. Hegel and Ernest Renan made much of the vaunted discovery of a God who did not yet exist but who was to be realized gradually (always the effective cause!) by Mankind. Indeed, the notion that has fascinated many dullards is but the counterfeit of what actually happened, according to the account handed down for generations through the children's catechism. I mean the Promise made to our first parents as they left the earthly Paradise, restated by Moses in the famous passage of Deuteronomy which literalists try in vain to water down, and triumphantly trumpeted by the prophets. *Mercy and Truth are met together,* said the psalmist; *righteousness and peace have kissed.* Hosea said: *I will hear the heavens, and they shall hear the earth.* And Isaiah said: *Drop down, ye heavens, from above, and let the skies pour down righteousness; let*

---

[3] *Post eum lucebit semina: their seed shall be established before thee.* (*Psalms* 102:28).

the earth open and bring forth salvation. And then was
heard the shout that was to echo endlessly throughout the
length and breadth of the land: *I have long time holden my
peace; I have been still, and refrained myself; now will I cry
like a travailing woman! It is I! I Come!* said the Virgin of
Nazareth. *Here am I.*

There is beauty and grandeur in the thought of a creature
laboring to give birth to a Savior. And no one can say that
He was not needed. Nothing holds a more profound truth
than St. Paul's words: *For we know that the whole creation
groaneth and travaileth in pain together until now; for the
earnest expectation of the creature waiteth for the manifestation of the sons of God.* Great leaders know that there is in
the heart of every human being a latent heroism that begs for
the opportunity to come forth. Psychoanalysts speak of *repression.* To be sure, repression exists, but not always as the
result of outer pressure. It is stronger when brought about
by an inner pressure, when the creature, who *was made subject to vanity, not willingly,* hears himself called by name
and throws off the bestial fetters of habit used in the attempt
to strangle him. "I am not of this world! I do not ask that my
strength be tapped. I ask that I be given the means to use my
strength. I ask to be needed. To fill an essential need. To be
needed as I am. Now that I exist, I must co-exist by applying
all my strength and will."

The capital importance of giving first place to the idea of
finality is now apparent. It gives *direction* to our lives and to
the history of Mankind to which we, too, have contributed.
No longer are we like slaves who work under the lash of the
tyrant. We are artists inspired by a leader who needs nothing
more than our freedom. Sweet freedom! A thousand times
more exacting than bondage. Our lives have taken on dignity
and worth. What dignity, good Lord, and what worth! We
have overcome the *vanity* lamented in the Book of Ecclesiastes. We can now make use of everything that helps us to

serve. We have eyes to look ahead, ears to detect whatever goes on around us, minds that enable us to understand, consciences for judging, memories for imagining, and everything else needed to carry out our wills. And beyond all that, as if continuously to temper everything, the harmonious feeling for music. *Make sweet melody,* says a verse of Scripture which sums up a whole system of ethics. And the exhortation has two meanings. First, do nothing to erase your feeling for the melodic line that allows you, personally, to re-establish your identity, in much the same way as an animal guided by instinct, amid conflicting outer pressures. Second, *watch and pray,* we are told by the Gospels, meaning that our music-stand has both an active and a passive role in the orchestral development. Passively within the sacred composition in which we are all notes, we are exhorted not to sin against the kind of *just-ness* that blends in with *justice.* This *Just-ness* (*Justum, just* in the abstract sense) must be brought into perfect harmony under the leadership of the choirmaster. And how desperately we are needed! A sudden silence on our part and a gaping hole large enough to swallow us rends the orchestra!

One life-span opens but a small, mediocre field to the melodic line in its contrapuntal development, to the past that gives meaning and direction to the future, and to the evocation of the new that brings to an end its well-ordered and inspired beginning. But the vast sweep of History since the birth of Christ, the horizon that has continued to expand before us, exerts an irresistible pull. The primordial commandment given to man *to till the soil* still rings in our ears. More is meant than the material process of breaking ground, in which both the sword and the plow have a role. More is meant than the rendering of services, the exploiting of resources, the dispensing of order and peace, and all the goods and services that result from the combined activities of the colonist, the engineer, the doctor, the magistrate and the policeman. *I am come,* said Christ, *that they might have life, and that they might have it more abundantly.* What is meant is the renewing, animating and illuminating of a latent being, of a brother whom we needed and who needed us, of a new face to listen to us, and of a new voice to answer us.

My life has not been wasted since I have been privileged to see the first fruits of the Christian harvest spring up all around me in the Far East. I recall, beside the abandoned pagodas of China, churches filled and packed with a solid, living mass of fervent men, women and children. I recall poor little Japanese mothers going to the Communion Table with their babies on their backs. I like the paintings that reflect the new themes contributed by the Gospel to a decadent art. Finally, the steeple-dotted landscapes of some parts of Indo-China seem just as Christian to me as the landscape of Brittany. Others could speak equally optimistically of apostolic work carried out in South America and Africa. This is no longer the time for melancholy and for all the other unpleasant thoughts of pagan pessimism!

In short, in the world there is continuing movement imprisoned in form: this is the kingdom of matter. There is cyclical movement in a form enslaved to repetition: this is the kingdom of living beings. And there is linear movement directed toward an end: this is human History.

We know from observation that the life of any particular animal is strictly regulated by its environment. From its surroundings, the animal must draw its subsistence. It must accordingly adapt itelf to a set pattern, though the remote and the unknown often are imposed at the expense of the immediate, as in the case of eels and migratory species. In man, even in the case of the most menial workers and of their most slavish needs, the present and the immediate are much less tyrannical. Man is now able to face, not just a few, but all situations, because instinct has been so largely replaced by intelligence, imagination and will. It can be said without ex-

aggeration that the future is the main motive force in man
and that his day is spent in planning for what is to come later
as seen in perspective. Take the peasant who seeds his field,
the laborer who works for a salary, the banker who opens a
credit account, the speculator who takes a long-term position,
or the diplomat who takes part in negotiations—the future
always takes first place and relegates the present to a mere
preparatory role. Everything happens as if we are to be swallowed up by the future which we must prepare for ourselves.

The main elements of the process are intelligence, judgment, experience and, to an even greater degree, the affec-
tive and emotional parts of our temperament. Nor should we
neglect strong pressures from within and without. But often,
whether under the pressure of time or as a result of the mysterious phenomenon called intuition, a lightning flash links
the thought and the act. In a moment I shall speak of scientific and poetic inspiration. But in general it can be said that
inspiration—which often is a transcendent interruption in
or adjunct to the routine course of our lives—has a basic, indispensable place in our psychological functioning. The
financier, the practicioner, the soldier, the policeman, the
mother and the lover—each is inspired. And of course it is
trite to point to the artist or writer and say that, even though
he has technical mastery, he is nothing unless he has "the
gift of the muse." Symbols, prosody and rime are not used to
mold thought but to stimulate it. In the same way, old English dramas introduced an incident which was not related to
the main theme, but which acted as a catalyst. Or some detail
of a painting is meaningless except for a touch of blue or
yellow (or something even more subtle). Or a certain feeling
which two people must have to achieve complete spiritual
harmony.

Here analogy, as formulated above by St. Bonaventure,
works its miracles as an instrument of discovery. Claude Bernard saw flies attacking some discarded bits of liver; as soon

as the fly-sugar association flashed through his mind, he discovered the glycogenic function of the liver. Charles Nicolle attributed his main discovery about typhus to the sight of a closed door. Victor Hugo looked at the head of a sheep and communicated the feeling of panic to us in his *Brebis Épouvante*. Mallarmé defined poetry as "the hymn of the relations between everything and the whole." The Bible repeatedly tells us to *ask now the beasts,* and every creature of God in general, thus introducing us to spiritual depths which would otherwise have been denied us. I compare such flashes of insight to the reward of a child who searches for Napoleon's head somewhere in a picture puzzle, then blinks his eyes and suddenly sees it standing out from the maze of foliage in front of him. Another comparison: radar. Simultaneously we send and receive waves and echoes. The psalmist tells us that faith sharpens our hearing.

Finally, after this long disquisition, we are in a better position to judge *inspiration* and *prophecy,* the spirit that animated the authors of the Sacred Books. *Gratia,*[4] says the adage, *perficit naturam,* meaning that divine love first purifies nature, then crowns it. Just as the Creator's left hand makes it possible for His creature to carry out the commandment of His right, and just as the earth and sea were placed in a position to honor the demand made upon them by plants, animals and man, so History has something called *generations*—a human growth which a woman's womb prepared for its vocation, which was the evocation of a face with a name. There is an obvious kinship of temperament between the men of the French Revolution and the men of the Russian Revolution, between the men of the First Empire and the Second Empire, and between all the isolated Prometheans of the nineteenth century: Goethe, Balzac, Hugo, Darwin,

---

[4] That the gift of prophecy is not inseparable from holiness is proven by the cases of Balaam and Caiaphas. Without charity, the gift of prophecy is useless. See I *Corinthians* 13:2.

Karl Marx, Bismarck, Wagner, Lesseps, Pasteur, Disraeli, Tolstoy, Ibsen, Rodin and Liszt. In the Book of Isaiah, there is a remarkable sentence which was uttered by the prophet and addressed to Jerusalem: *Ye shall conceive heat, ye shall bring forth stubble; your breath, as fire, shall devour you.* It might seem more logical to reverse the order and put the fuel before the spark. Here, on the contrary, the spark within the woman kindles the substance before making it burst into flame. In the same way inspiration and aspiration are kindled by the Inspired. When the apostles gathered together in Jerusalem after a retreat of ten days, the Holy Spirit fell upon them. They were quick to respond to His presence: the flame which was rooted in their entrails brightened their countenances! How many different ways there are for four lips which exhale two streams of breath to communicate! Habakkuk the reaper struggled in the hands of an inspired angel, and Jonah fought with all his might against the wings that tried to wrest him from the earth. Against this, Jeremiah was chosen from the moment of his conception, and Isaiah is shown, pen in hand, surrounded by the Trinity. How many saintly women pay for his prophecy through the long sterility required of them by the Scriptures! But to come back to profane examples: think of all the converging circumstances and events necessary to explain how a talented author uses his resources to produce the Iliad or the Aeneid, or Phèdre or Hamlet!

Let Him kiss me with the kisses of His mouth! This unheard-of cry right in the middle of the Old Testament was nurtured in the hearts of generations before it erupted from the lips of Solomon's bride in answer to her Savior's command: *Thou shalt love the Lord thy God with all thine heart, and with all thy soul, and with all thy might.* And through the literal statements of the prophets, God speaks in turn. *I shall wed thee in justice!* said Hosea. And Isaiah: *Can a woman forget her suckling child? Yea, they may forget, yet will I not forget thee. As I live, saith the Lord* (these are the words used to seal a promise) *thou shalt surely clothe thee as a bride!* And the dialogue between the Soul and Its Divine Lover soon continues. Since you need justice, *draw me!* says the Soul. *Trahe me!* for alone I am helpless. Let Thy left hand help me to carry out the will of Thy right hand! When struck down on the road to Damascus, St. Paul's immediate response was: *Lord, what wilt Thou have me to do?* After leaving him in darkness for a moment, God restored his sight as he had once purified Isaiah's lips. *I will shew him how great things he must suffer for My sake,* He said. *Suffer,* meaning to take upon his shoulders. Everything which his senses communicate to him and from which he will have to abstract Proofs.

Of course not everyone is privileged to be an Isaiah or a St. Paul. But Mankind has always furnished a number of specimens to fill in a pattern which scattered traits of the "rank and file" could only adumbrate. That is why proper names like Napoleon, Virgil, and Tartuffe pass into general usage as common nouns. And for the same reason vocations are rare but *temptations* are common. To be sure, immediate temptations are stronger and more common. But none of us has been denied the right to look straight across circumstances and draw a bead on the goal. In the language of the Scriptures, such sightings are called *arrows.* One of the prophets tells us: *At the light of thine arrows they went.* And another, to show how desire gives wings to sight: *Whose arrows are sharp, and all their bows bent.* But we have only our bruised feet to follow the arrow in its headlong flight. How comforting to hear, and not only to hear but to have within us, someone in whom we have placed our trust and who says to us: *I am the way!*

CHAPTER VI

Fulgens Corona[1]

Once again, as two years ago, thanks to the kind insistence of Father Claude Roffat and the courtesy of His Eminence Cardinal Gerlier who is now presiding, this old poet has been invited to come before a gathering of his friends from Lyons and give testimony of his faith. Since this is the end of the Marian year, I draw courage from the fact that all voices join in praising the Mother of God in this town which has been consecrated to her. Perhaps the sound of my voice is not wholly unknown to her since we met in the Cathedral of Notre Dame in Paris on a certain Christmas Day sixty-eight years ago. I have been dealing with her for so long and in so many ways that she has become part of every moment of my life; besides being familiar with every step of my long and full existence, she also knows my heart. Now is the time to allow this heart, before ceasing, to speak and to speak openly! To allow it to speak of her. That is what I have been asked to do this evening.

The first words that come to my lips are those that open His Holiness the Pope's encyclical on the Marian year: *Fulgens Corona.* A resplendent crown. A crown is what she

[1] Address delivered before the students of the Versailles Seminary on March 15, 1954.

is, a crown is what she receives, and a crown is what she determines. The royal crown which the Pope, in instituting a new Church festival, has solemnly placed on the brow of the Mother of God.

In Chapter 4 of the Song of Songs, God addresses the mysterious bride in whom the Church has always recognized the Sacred Virgin, saying: *Come with me from Lebanon, my spouse, thou shalt be crowned.* Lebanon, which means whiteness, suggests the Immaculate Conception. And St. John, in Chapter 12 of the Apocalypse, shows us the one who constitutes *a great wonder in heaven,* a woman clothed in sunlight and crowned with twelve stars. Twelve stands for fulness. This number recalls the twelve tribes of Israel and symbolizes the heavens on All Saint's Day in this year of grace nineteen hundred and fifty-four, the very day when the dogma of the Assumption was proclaimed. Each of these stars, each of these "luminous agents of space" of which old Aeschylus speaks, is indebted to Mary for its refulgence. "Bountiful virgin," says the prophet, "then shalt thou abound and be marveled at among the torrential people to whom thou hast given birth on one and the same day! Look upon those who come from the north and from the south! For not one of these radiant dwellers of eternity fails to look upon thee as his mother."

Her crown was an exacting crown. From human multitudes who tramped and stumbled piteously in the darkness, there swelled a question, and no mouth offered a satisfactory answer: "Who will make saints of us? Who will free the forces of knowledge, grace and action now locked in us?" And at the same time God, seeing in the endless sweep of the ages the countless number of His saints and His elected ones, asked: "Who will make me their father? Who will open the door? Who will open it for me? The way to mercy, which will be the inseparable companion of Justice?"

Then appeared Mary; the hour had come. She said yes.

She gave God to Mankind and she gave Mankind to God. She filled both longings. The prophet Hosea said that she provided wheat, wine and oil, the elements of the sacrament.

To provide these elements was to crown. And it is true, Mary is a crown. The Lorettan litanies tell us that she is also a door. A door is that which serves both sides as an entrance. And in the same way a crown has two sides in that it is the result as well as the cause of a union. The crown is not simply a decorative adjunct. Nor is it simply a sign or the sign of fulfilment. Of fulfilment it is both the instrument and the outcome. That is why the Song says that the Woman of whom we were just speaking rose like the trunk of a palm-tree whose boughs are arched by the weight of its fruit.

The fulfilment or the crown for each being is the perfection befitting him. Now the perfection of Mary is in being a servant, *ancilla Domini*. The devil said: *Non serviam*. But Mary wished only to be a servant and to render service. Since God used so many imperfect instruments, He could not fail to make use of this perfect one whom He himself called: *Perfecta mea*. She served by being a mother, and as a perfect servant she was a perfect mother. Giving birth to children was not her sole function. She did not stop exercising her maternity until they reached fulfilment in the crown.

To serve is not to create, but to administer. To administer for God in all that befalls us impatient creatures of flesh and blood by virtue of our being sons of God. The prophet Zechariah calls God a Branch. We are sons of God, hence must have within us a branch of God. Mary is aware of this branch which we share through her. Just as she implanted it in us, so she cares for it, cultivates in us the vocation of the crown itself. And she is that crown. Not merely a decorative crown: an organic cluster which allows us full self-realization and, if I may say so, full birth in the sight of our Creator. It allows us to experience actual birth.

Which of Mary's crowns? I need only follow the description given by the Jesuit Father Porée. It is a triple crown. There are, he says, the crown of signification, the crown of glory and the crown of beneficence.

Signification here has its usual meaning. It is a word which sums up the whole person and focuses our attention on the present. It focuses our attention in order that we may reply. Mary is the full answer, in the name of humanity, to the call of God, the ancient *Where art thou?* which rang out through the Garden of Eden after the Fall.

"Where art thou?" asked an anguished Father. Nor could the blind creature, who was the unwilling subject of vanity, manage to suppress the hopeless question that came to her lips: "Thou, Father, where art thou?" All that was necessary was that someone show us our Father. And then a shout rang out: "I have found Him! *I have found Him and I will not let Him go* (*Songs* 6)! I have found Him, and He will never be able to rid Himself of me! I have Him, I hold Him, I enfold Him, or rather He enfolds me. How shall I say it? In the presence of the nations I am the stem from which he takes root, stature, life, countenance, speech. Surely you have heard the voice from heaven which said: *This is my well-beloved Son. Hear ye Him!* It is I also who have the right to say: This one, this well-beloved son, He is also mine. From me He received breath and speech and the right to say to you: *Whosoever sees Me sees My Father.*" Speech, which is the Word, was now in one soul and one body. Not a passing sound, but someone who was with us to stay until the end of time. "Here is the One whom I begat to give signification to everything, the One through whom nothing exists without being a sign and an allusion, the One who gave His name to Creation because He was the beginning and the end. I have put Him at your disposal. Receive Him! Behold Him! And if you cannot bear Him, I give you my face. Behold me as I behold Him! Behold the face of the mother who made Him."

That is the crown of signification. What is the crown of

glory? Glory is the exclusive attribute of God, as we are told in the Epistle to the Romans (16:27): *To God only be glory through Jesus Christ!* and in Isaiah (42:8): *I am the Lord: that is my name; and my glory will I not give to another.*

This does not mean that He reserves His glory jealously for Himself while we hear daily at mass that it fills heaven and the earth. But it does mean that He alone is the authentic dispenser of glory, just as He alone is worthy of glory. For this reason the Apocalypse shows Him being crowned with many diadems while the twenty-four prostrate old men throw their crowns at His feet. Though His crown belonged to Him by eternal right, He preferred to merit it through Righteousness in accordance with the word of Isaiah (61:10): *He hath covered me with the robe of righteousness* (referring to the flesh which He has put on) *as a bridegroom decketh himself with ornaments.* But who gave Him the robe of righteousness? Who allowed him to merit glory? The Song of Solomon gives the answer (3:11): *Go forth, O ye daughters of Zion, and behold king Solomon with the crown wherewith his mother crowned him in the day of the gladness of his heart.* And indeed, we are told by St. John (19:5) that *Jesus came forth*—He came forth to meet His Father, and also us—*wearing the crown of thorns.* Would He not share with His Mother this merited crown of righteousness and glory which He owed to her? Worshipers generally picture their two hearts enveloped by the same triumphant thorn. We read in the Book of Kings (I, 8:11) that *the Glory of the Lord had filled the house of the Lord.* What is to be said of the golden House which never ceased reflecting the rays of Nazareth and of Calvary? *Gold is mine, saith the Lord* (*Haggai* 2:8), but Mary is pure gold, a mirror, a ray, purity, fidelity. It is she whom the Song of Solomon compares to a perfect, immaculate moon. No part of the ray which she received does she keep for herself. But it cannot be said that she casts it out. No, for we are told that she keeps in her heart all the things that she received from God, and that all the glory of the Daughter of the King comes from within. By preserving she is serving. It is she, the strong Woman, who serves God, renders service to God and makes use of God. It is she who collates all things in her heart. She gives the finishing touch to all Creation and offers it as a crown of glory to God. She explains God to creation and, I might even say, explains Creation to God through the "condensed consummation" which she is. It is good to give praise to God! It is good to have become the sons of God through such a mother as she! It is good for us all to be the sons of God and to need each other in order for all of us to form a crown of glory around God through such a Mother as she! An inextricable crown! It is good to learn from her how to understand ourselves as creatures of God, how to compare ourselves with others only with respect to the qualities we share as creatures of God, and how to use God only in order to serve God. *Yet of myself I will not glory, but in mine infirmities,* said the Apostle. That is, in the ways given me to have need of my Creator, I will glorify Him.

And that is how, like the colors of the rainbow, the crown of glory blends into the crown of beneficence.

When, on the eve of Calvary, Magdalena came prayerfully with her alabaster jar and spilled tears over the feet of the Saviour, there was a scent comparable to the mysterious sound of Holy Ghost which, according to the Acts of the Apostles, suddenly filled the whole house. Now was the time for the sacred spikenard of which we are told in the Song of Songs to give forth its powerful sweet smell. Similarly, when the substantial recognition takes place between the Husband of souls and some happily chosen creature, we should not be surprised to find that, when the deepest bond is severed, a scent fills the whole house and the tidings are immediately spread far and wide. Powerful, compelling tidings indeed! For though it is possible to resist an argument, who could resist a sweet smell? Who could resist this scent which, according to St. Paul, is *the sweet savor of Christ?* But that which is the precarious reward of a few privileged minutes to us here below is a permanent attribute of the Righteousness that is shared by the Virgin and her Husband and Son; its emanation spreads throughout the earth, throughout creation. And such is, I am sure, the crown of beneficence of which Father Porée speaks. A life-giving crown, not for mere sensual pleasure, but something nourishing and wholesome, which will surely grant humility and patience as well as the higher gifts of courage and character.

The last word has not yet been said. To pay homage to the Virgin in thought and by words of praise is not enough. We must co-operate with her; we must be ready to test and find out through deeds just what we mean to her and she to us in order really to become one.

St. Paul's first words on meeting his Savior on the road to Damascus were: *Lord, what wilt thou have me to do?* In a word, He is the being and substance of the Virgin, who is only a servant who serves, works and earns, and who is so close to us that she could not keep from communicating to us her zeal for serving and working and earning. Behold her facing her Son as she shows Him the encircling sky, not the sky of passing stars but the sky of souls that are constantly born and reborn in the sun of Truth, and says to him: "I was not barren in thy hands! See what I have made of Thee! See what I have made of Thee with Thee! See all that I have given Thee since the call was addressed to me saying: 'Hearken, my daughter!' The call of which I was made and which said to me: 'Fear not! Ask!' I asked! I have multiplied. Around Thee are the numberless generations of this Mary who said yes and who never stops adding to Thy crown, O God, and to mine, through acceptance of my role. O God, how is it possible for Thee to escape from the net which I have cast around Thee? Thou art now the prey, as we are told by the prophet, of the exultant hunters! It is better, Thou hast said, to give than to receive. That is why Thou hast chosen to use me to extend to all Thy children the privilege of beneficence which I exemplify. Thou art the lasting fare which they share with each other. Thou, their master, hast knelt before them as a beggar in order that they might have something to give to Thee and to each other."

What words did the prodigal Son hear spoken when, clinging to His Father and letting His head drop on His shoulder, there was only a short distance between his humbled ear and the whispering mouth? *Omnia mea tua sunt.* And no mere show of affection prompted Christ at Calvary, when He named Mankind as His heir in His will, to bequeath a son to His mother and a mother—His mother—to the son; the act was solemn, sacramental. The son He bequeathed with all the needs that tax every thread of motherhood, and the mother—His mother—he bequeathed with all her privileges. One was told to watch over, the other to watch. By watching, one reaches a state of contemplation, and contemplation yields understanding. Thus when certain afflictions come upon us—as when we have lost a loved one—during our first state of shock and stupefaction we might be said to feel nothing; later, when someone nearby breaks down and cries, our hearts explode in the sudden realization of our loss. Similarly, at a concert we listen to the work of a great musician, but nothing happens. We are deaf to the music until we catch sight of a face close to our own—a face radiant with understanding and feeling—then deep within us a kindred ear opens to the sublime strains.

Through contemplation, which is a long, intensive look, I said that we reach understanding. A lady whose perceptiveness was greatly admired once said: "When two people are talking in a room, if I want to find out what they are saying, I imitate their facial expressions and the movements of their lips." She needed only a brief, superficial contact. But here, more is demanded of us. Through understanding we reach communion, and through communion, likeness.

But what possible likeness is there, it might be argued, between us and the Mother of God? We must clearly understand that Mary is not a special creation of the Almighty whose likeness to Mankind is restricted to her outward appearance. On the contrary, we read that she was elected, that she was chosen, and that she was blessed among all women. This means that she was not only a woman but also the paragon of womanhood and that she typifies the ideal of a child-bearing woman that has been an object of search and fulfilment, of realization and crowning, for succeeding generations. Though she was singled out from among all the people to whom she had been joined, she remained a part of them. *Una est electa mea,* says the Song of Songs. The result is that, just as all fatherhood is in God, so all motherhood is in Mary; she was chosen as the guardian of the motherhood which is in Him in accordance with the words that the prophet Isaiah put into His mouth: *Can a woman forget her suckling child? Yea, yet will I not forget Thee.* Mary became the mother of Jesus Christ, which means that all women crowned by her and joined together through her have become in a certain sense the mothers of Jesus Christ. "Daughter of Eve, the whole one born of thee, who art a woman among all women," said the Angel, "will be called the Son of God. Behold, He comes from the deepest entrails of mankind."

Every man worthy of the name realizes that he is, as St. James said, but the vague beginning of a creature. He is but the outline of the being, the mysterious I, whose development God entrusted to negative and rational forces. Pagan philosophers, both past and present, imagined that this development would come from without and through their own efforts. "Make a statue," said the proud men of the Portico. Hear how the prophet Isaiah ridicules statues and the makers of idols: *The smith with the tongs both worketh in the coals,*

*and fashioneth it with hammers, a little here and a little there.
Modicum ibi, modicum ibi. The carpenter stretcheth out his
rule; he marketh it out with a line; he fitteth it with planes,
and he marketh it out with the compass, and maketh it after
the figure of a man, according to the beauty of a man; that it
may remain in the house.* You know the result. You need
only turn to Plutarch's *Lives of Great Men,* or to the bronze
idols that once adorned our streets. But all the activity mentioned by Isaiah is really quite tiring. It is simpler, following
the advice of Kant—advice followed by newspaper dupes fascinated by their own navels—to build our shortcomings into a
universal maxim and thereby to obtain something comparable to the products of Negro art which are currently in vogue.
What man, asks the Gospel, can add one cubit to his stature,
even if he tries to lift himself out of his boots by pulling on his
hair?

The important thing is not for man to make an idol of and
by himself but for him to give fulfilment to the *branch,* as
described earlier in the words of Zechariah, which God implanted in us in order to produce someone in His image. This
seminal vocation is what Jesus entrusted to His mother whose
functions the Church assumed in order to insure her support
and nourishment. *Woman,* we read in the Gospel, *What
have I to do with thee?* What? Fatherhood and Motherhood.
Through motherhood God became the son of man, and
through motherhood man became the son of God, as we learn
from Jesus, who told Nicodemus that he *must be born
again.* When we learn that this sage—this astounded literalist
—asked if he had to enter the womb of his mother again, we
think of all the generations which a certain mother held in
her womb and which the Church will continue to bring forth
into the light of the sun until the end of time. Here God en-
lists in his service a new kind of womanhood, one born of a
mother. It is not in vain that in many parts of our country
Mary is invoked under the name of Our Lady of Deliverance.

She does deliver us. Deep within every human being there is a captive, hidden soul who is the unwilling subject of vanity and who blindly aspires to knowledge and light. But she would never have succeeded in saying yes or in winning her woeful struggle against darkness and oppression without the help of the representative of the Church, which is inseparable from the daughter of Anne and Joakim, in her obstetrical labor. *Thou hast put off my sackcloth,* says the Psalm—the hideous sackcloth that imprisoned me—*and girded me with gladness.* Finally a golden hand had been placed on us! The Church generously fills our mental and spiritual needs, as well as our need for beauty, truth, love—for everything that makes it possible for us to rise up from the depths of our congenital frustration and respond to the heart-breaking appeals of the sorrowful world around us. "Come," says the Church, "and drink abundantly!"

Dear friends, I did not come here to deliver a sermon. That would be, as the English proverb puts it, like carrying coals to Newcastle. I am merely taking advantage of the opportunity afforded me to assuage my heart and to give vent to some of the feelings which I have had to keep repressed and buried deep inside me all my life. Loneliness is the testing ground of many priests; it can also afflict us when we are surrounded by people with whom we feel that we have very little in common. No one has understood better than I the words of Saint Paul when he spoke of using the world as if one were not using it, not through virtue but through unpleasant necessity. Many times a dinner-jacket has seemed like a sackcloth to me. Then I would have preferred a high rock in the middle of the Pacific Ocean to the chair of honor at an official dinner where I had to put my rosary under the tablecloth between the wives of two American senators. Indeed to the loneliness that traveled with me was added the loneliness of exile, for my whole life was spent among people whose language, interests and religion differed from mine. I also suffered from the loneliness of a writer who devotes himself despairingly to his art; though he knows that no one will understand him, he continues to fight against the double standards of two equally indifferent and opposing walls. It was then that I again realized the worth throughout the four corners of the world of this mother who had once borne me and had not let me go. Everywhere I was able to find a Catholic church which opened its doors to me. Not the matchless vaults of Notre Dame of Paris, but some poor shanty in a missionary region or some humble asylum of the poor—painfully and proudly aware of its humility—at the end of a narrow street in Boston or Hamburg. Regardless of its appearance, I looked upon it as the house of gold of the litanies—which our parishioners translate as charitable sanctuary—the gate to heaven or the bridging arch above which shone the morning star, the very star which the priest was to put into my mouth.

Not only did Providence put havens along my route; she also provided priests. The first of these, Father Vuillaume, Vicar of Saint-Médard, had a profound influence on my development. He was a strict man who understood from the outset how to exact obedience from the unruly youth that I was at that time. It was he who forced me, despite my reluctance, to join the Society of Saint Vincent de Paul. He also introduced me to Planchat Street, where I met Father Anizan. He also was the one to whom I am deeply indebted for having been forced to read, without preparation, the two *Summas* of St. Thomas, which were the backbone of my studies during my first five years in China. Later, I had the privilege of becoming acquainted with two eminent priests, Father Daniel Fontaine, rector of Clichy, and Father Mary, rector of Saint-Jean-les-deux-Jumeaux, both characterized by humility, cheerfulness, goodness and saintliness. Their influence on me, though edifying, could not be compared to the wise, healthful, strong and cruel hand of Father Vuillaume, which was the very thing that I needed during that period of my life. For there is where

I first understood, from the human point of view, the bonds of austere affection that can grow up between a penitent and his guide.

I am speaking from the human point of view. Later, in the course of a long and varied career, I rarely dealt with anyone other than unknown and unseen priests from whom I was also kept apart by language and with whom I could have only a sacramental relationship. The situation scarcely changed in France during the war years. In the village which sheltered me, I found behind the screen of the confessional a droll old priest whose stammering cut through the silence without much effect, for he was addressing a deaf person. That is the human point of view; but this casual priest, unknown and unseen but acting in his sacramental role, realized the good that he was doing and the great, awesome power residing in him when over the corrupt one kneeling before him with the hideous taste of mortal or venial sin in his mouth he held the hand that absolved him *ex omni vinculo excommunicationis et interdicti*, and saw a free man arise unburdened, enlightened and garbed in pristine innocence.

The same hand put the small white host on his tongue the next morning. This is the hand referred to in the Song of Songs; it is the hand that distills myrrh and reaches through the opening of this meager world to give us refreshment. There was always a priest—whether in China, Japan, Brazil, predominately Protestant areas of Germany and America, or Bordeaux and Algeria marred by darkest humiliation and defeat—to lift up the thin wafer held between his fingers and ask us if we were worthy of receiving it. Worthy, Father? Worthy, do you say? Of course we are not worthy, but this does not keep us from joining the vast waves of believers who belong to all races, tribes and tongues of mankind and to all classes and ages, and who surge one after the other around the communion table to open the deepest recesses of their mouths and hearts to their sole Savior—to the sole Beloved who no longer speaks to them in proverbs. *Open up thy heart,* says the psalm, *and thou shalt be filled . . .*

The heavens above me have changed many times, but in them I have never failed to find Mary or the Church; around me I have never failed to find the bright-pointed crown, which is the constant and beneficent guide that keeps me on the straight and narrow path.

And how marvelous! Mary took the crown from her brow and gave it to us to use as an instrument of contemplation and efficacy. We call it the Rosary. The little bead held between the thumb and index finger is Mary herself; she becomes the vehicle of our eyes and voices and carries us along the path of worship in a cycle that is endlessly repeated. Mary, the Church and the Mother of God is placed in our hands for our use. "Hear my cry, O Lord!" we read throughout the Psalms, "Hear my voice! Do not fall asleep!" Day and night the muffled din, punctuated by piercing cries, rises from the earth toward God! A growing wave of Hail Mary's which never allows Him to sleep.

But there is another crown, or let us say rather a net. One Christmas evening in Notre Dame, the divine hunter caught me and held me in this net until the day when, almost at the end of my long life, I crossed the railing of the choir and chanced, at the feet of venerable canons, to find myself fully at ease and in my place. I am speaking of the liturgy; the spiritual zodiac whose twelve Houses are occupied in succession by the sun is the revolving table where the Church comes to present the bountiful fruits of Grace to God and gradually to prepare for the rewards of eternity through the fulness of work accomplished and the sealed promise. Somewhere deep within a pagan or Protestant town, there was always someone who, imperturbable and indifferent to the secular uproar, turned the pages of his breviary one by one.

Liturgy, as I understand it today, is not an inviolable sanc-

tuary that serves us as a refuge against the cruelties and of-
fenses of a world which, as St. John tells us, *is beset by Evil.*
The Church is the crowning of Mankind, as Mankind is the
crowning of nature. Both are instruments of divine worship,
and that is why the Psalms tell us that *God crowns the year
with His goodness.* I once dreamed of dedicating my life to
the *opus Dei* in a monastery; this dream had its place in my
lay existence. It enabled me to keep my mind on my work,
and to guard against frivolity, ignorance and deceit. For on
the outside I was to find a copy of what I had been taught
to read within a monastery. Gradually I became convinced
that there is no lay world where redemption figures as an
alien episode, but that Christ is really the alpha and the
omega; nothing exists except by and for Christ; every single
detail of time and nature converges on Christ from the four
points of the horizon; everything converges on Christ crucified or, as we are told in a vital text of the Book of Revelations,
the lamb slain from the foundation of the world. The Epistle
to the Hebrews tells us that the Christ of the Cross was *appointed heir of all things.* My heart-felt need of Christ was the
need of the whole world which seeks to free itself from vanity
and to find direction and meaning, not through redemption,
but through something else. "Where is your God?" asked a
voice that echoed to the ends of the earth. Then I recalled the
book where once, long before, on the knees of Our Lady, I had
learned to spell out the rudiments. I was sixty years old when
I heard that question. The hour of retirement was about to
strike for me. I had been told that this book—and experience
had borne this out—was the Word of God, the written Word.
How fascinating, the Word of God! Why not, in the future,
devote my life to it? The hour of delight had passed; another,
the hour of love and study, had come.

The hour to be catholic. My hour had come; I was given the
opportunity which I had coveted since the day of my con-
version; I was given the opportunity to become catholic in the

universal sense: someone who has really climbed above the world and no longer sees in it anything alien to Christ, even in contradiction, wrong or sin. Someone who has climbed and been made to climb the mountain of purity, which is also the mountain of revelation mentioned in this verse of the Song of Songs: *Come with me from Lebanon, and thou shalt be crowned.* Someone who stands on the peak of a mountain and looks down at his feet and sees the earth crowning him and converging on him. The Church Fathers were not wrong in seeking only Christ in the Scriptures and in looking on everything else as vanity. And, indeed, *multifariam multisque modis,* St. Paul tells us, sometimes openly, sometimes by inference, sometimes by direct order, and sometimes by a distant allusion or an echo reflected by many walls, that nothing in the world exists or happens except through Christ and the Lamb that was sacrificed, according to the Book of Revelation, before the creation of the world. Everything that exists is a symbol, and everything that happens is a parable. The Scriptures are both a lexicon and a narration of events. The lexicon includes no abstract terms; its alphabet is made up of elements that owe their existence, which is a true existence, to a divine fiat and not to any fiat of man. Ask the animate beings, the Book of Job tells us, and also those that are not animate. Everything contains an image which roughly approximates divine energies and perfections, and which I shall call a sacramental image. This is true of earth, sea, mountains, flowers, plants, animals, wine, wheat, oil, a lamp, a door, an arm, a vase, or even the basest of objects. Sacred objects. The same holds for all the feelings and interpersonal relations that give but a faint hint of what true marriage and fatherhood or true friendship and fellowship really are. And as for events, the heart of the Scriptures is the preparation, narration and elucidation for all the ages of the supreme event, the Advent of Man and the Son of God through whom all things—yes, that is the right expression—all things are reconciled in heaven and on earth. Everything else is but the frivolous and often pernicious pastime of scholars who would do well to mull over the words of an ancient Jew, Rabbi Eleazar: "Accursed be he who pretends that the statements of the Scriptures have only their literal sense. For, if that were true, the Scriptures would not be the Law of truth, the holy Law and the heavenly Law. Even a king of flesh and bone would think it beneath his dignity to say trivial things or, with even more justification, to write them. The King on High—the Holy of Holies, bless His name—certainly could have found something holier than a collection of simple stories to formulate His law. The stories of Esau, Agar, Laban, the ass of Balaam, Balak, Zamzi and the like are not enough to justify calling the Scriptures Truth, perfect Law, testimonial Law, and 'Law more precious than gold and all the mysteries.' "

But Pascal, in commenting on St. Denys, tells us that the coarser the appearance or rough outer dress of the two prophets of the Apocalypse, the more carefully we should search beneath for the priceless truth hidden there.

A short while ago I spoke of the crown of signification. This crown covers the woman who, according to St. John, is garbed in sunlight—that is, in the powerful light that makes it possible for us to see everything, penetrate everything, and understand everything. On her head glistens the supreme gem of her resplendent crown, of the *fulgens corona* which we may nourish the hope of seeing one day beside the mystic rose and the house of gold found among the invocations of the litany. It has been said that many saints and religious men, particularly St. Bernard, literally knew the Scriptures by heart, like the thousand shields which adorned the walls of King David's mystic arsenal and vibrated to the sound of his harp, and that verses rushed to their lips to fulfill their spiritual and emotional needs and to solve all the problems of daily life for them. But the Blessed Virgin did not need to learn the Bible; she is a living Bible; she supports the Word;

she is the trunk of the sun that enlightens the world through the radiation of words which do not pass away. She stands there, singing the Magnificat and telling God the great things that He has seen fit to do for her. She is the voice of the fulness of the pregnant universe which encircles her like a crown and which she relieves of the great need of bearing witness and of giving thanks.

Here is the Lord's servant, says she. See how the servant has served! She has served God; she has been of service to God. See how even Satan, the renegade who boasted that he would serve no person or purpose, is now, at long last, held fast under hard talons; as we are told in the Epistle to the Philippians, he too serves. Wrong served, suffering served, sin served, hell served; everything worked together on this exalted cross on which Mary's Son gloriously died! And I, a poor old man who has never served any purpose, who was never in his life capable of thinking about the same thing for ten minutes in succession, how happy I am to have Mary in heaven to tell God all the good things that I think about him! And how grateful I am to the poor priest there in Rome who was asking his Master from his sickbed for the right to suffer and work still a little while for Him and for His children just as I was writing these lines, for having raised Mary to perfection on the highest throne of heaven and crowned her! In flesh as in spirit. The one whom the Song of Songs calls whole and perfect. Whole, perfect in order that we may hold out our arms to her. *Assumpta est Maria ad aethereum thalamum in Rex regum Stellato sedit solis. Veni, coronaberis!*

CHAPTER VII

Evil Before Original Sin

The creation of the world, according to a well established tradition, is tied to the secession of the bad Angels, the evocation of the Blessed Virgin, and the proposal of an incarnation; the means of the incarnation was implied in the underlying cause. The revolt did not free the angels from serving, for the very essence and function of Angels, which are *administratorii spiritus*, is to serve. A short while before they had been good; now they were evil. Well, God has the power to make use of evil also. The devil can carry stone, as they say. There was no reason for the architect to deprive himself of the talents of any of these masters of second causes.

And then the old question at the crux of our thought and being again comes up for debate. Since God exists, why must anything else exist? Since He alone exists, how can there be something which—because it is not He—cannot be that which is not? And if love explains communion, how can there be communion apart from cognition and recognition? Why the impervious interposition of second causes between the creature and his first Cause? Why this creature whose essence is in proving that he exists apart from God? Suppose that someone says that God the absolute Good does not exist, or pretends that something can exist apart from God, or proclaims

that something is free and independent. The only possible explanation is evil. For God who is absolute Good can not will
evil. Evil can result only from the intervention of an alien
will, an enemy, or the one whom the Gospels call the Evil One
and the Wicked One.

That the intervention of the Evil One played a part in the
creation of the world is proved by the Gospel, which constantly refers to the devil as *Prince of this world*. St. Paul calls
him *the power of darkness*. St. John tells us that *the whole
world is beset by Evil*. And on Holy Saturday we are struck
by the exorcisms which the priest performs above the *holy
water*, as if to rid it of the bad element infused into it. Adam's
sin merely aggravated but did not explain the general in-
festation of nature. Before Adam's sin there was physical evil
and—as a necessary and integral part of the general plan—the
suffering and death which the Apocalypse calls the supreme
enemy, the first death, which symbolizes *the second death*.
Thus God assumes exclusive responsibility for neither
Behemoth and Leviathan nor the creation of the pests and
mites, wolves and leprosy, tuberculosis and all the other fear-
fully insidious ills that beset and torture animal flesh.

The Apocalypse tells us that the Lamb *was slain from the
foundation of the world*. Thus there was something which had
required the spilling of this redeeming blood since the creation of the world.

The Gospel completes our enlightenment. For we read in
St. John (12:32): *And I, if I be lifted up from the earth,
will draw all men unto Me.* But we have just read that before
the creation of the world, *the Lamb was slain*, that is, that He
was raised on the cross and that as a result He does draw all
men unto Him. The world was created solely to prepare
for and participate in the Mass of the *heir of all things* (*Hebrews* 1:2). From the most remote point of eternity an order
went out to the ages, and still today this order is heard. Everything has acquired a purpose and *meaning*. Everything has

moved toward Christ; it has moved toward Christ made manifest in the womb of Mary and made manifest until the end of time in the body of which we are parts. The Epistle to the Hebrews makes no exceptions: Christ is the heir of all things, *universorum*, of the evil as well as the good. The order which was sent out to the world and which He inherited, was directed to all administrative powers, *administratorii spiritus;* it was directed to the good ones as well as to the bad ones about whose chief it was to be said later: *vade post me, get thee behind me.* They drew lots. Christ drew the world. The future drew the matter which was provided for it and which was to be given some measure of freedom in assuming the shape required of it.

The symphony was conceived and developed in our presence. It is wonderful to be seated near the composer and to have him carefully turn the pages of the score for us, one by one! *Universorum!* No instrument is excluded. All resources are put to some use. St. Paul tells us that *all things work together for good (Romans 8:28).* What about God himself? All resources are put to some use. Contradiction plays a role just as agreement does. Violence is always tempered by a mitigating force. And always the forward flight symbolized in the flight of the woman before the dragon. To her shoulders are attached the two wings of invention. Apollo's struggle against the Titans was not restricted to mythological times. It began with the world to continue until this day and until the Last Judgment. History simply follows prehistory. The world shows us nothing for which our hearts have not prepared us.

The first chapter of the Book of Genesis tells us that God ordered that there be light (the Latin word is *fieri;* God ordered light *to be made* or *to exist*). That light was not the eternal light but something created. We might call it the light that allowed God to see something apart from Himself. God does not say that after having created light He created darkness, or that from the light he separated the darkness; He says that he divided the light from the darkness (*Genesis* 1:4). This implies that darkness came first and that it may have resulted from the revolt of Satan. The revolt explains why *after* points to *before*, which is the beginning of time, and why through an apparent anomaly but in conformity with the Bible, Hebrew divides the day, not into morning and evening, but into evening (vespers) and morning. In negation Satan managed to carve out for himself an appanage apart from God. But God gives him no respite. To no avail he had imagined that Being would never be able to see something that does not exist. To no avail he conjures up nothingness. Only through unrelenting effort can he sustain himself apart from God. He is not allowed to exist but only to resist, to persist, to keep trying, to persevere in his refusal and to continue. But then we are struck forcibly by the thought of time, for it owes its distinctive trait, its passage, to something which is not. Light too—the light that comes out of darkness, keeps coming out of darkness, and enables darkness to obtain for itself a vision of something that is not—is also continuous and persistent. The movement created by the passage of visibility is like the movement of a dynamo around non-movement, and God enslaved that enormous dynamo. *The light shineth in darkness,* says the Gospel of St. John. The darkness is a screen, like the retina, on which images are painted. Light can impart colors ranging from the softest to the most intense hues, to these images. *God saw,* or perceived, *that the light was good.* And whatever is good in the eyes of God must be good for something and serve Him in some way. He used the light for something with respect to the darkness from which he had taken pains to divide it. *And the evening and the morning were* the first day. Using the darkness, God kindled in it something which prohibits rest, which goads it, which eats away on it (like an acid, which is the bite of Hosea), and which uses passive resistance to force it into active resistance. The devil uses time to flee, and God uses time to pursue him.

One look is enough. Please! Just open your eyes for a second! Not even on this very day is there serenity and peace in the moral and human world, but rather war and violence. Nor was the creation of the physical world attended by serenity and peace, but rather by unparalleled combat and violence. Nature is still a victim of extreme convulsions, of pains resembling those of childbirth. There are some sites in the Alps, and others in the Rocky Mountains, and still others in Tibet and in the Andean cordillera, which terrify us and cause us to cringe in horror; they produce an unmistakable impression of the Evil One. What cataclysms, what eruptions, what *bulls of Bashan among the kine of the people,* what desperate monsters clash, what defiance and blasphemy, and what maddening denials and short-term truces fall prey to hideous patience! But what happens resembles the plots of melodramas in which all excesses and all combinations of wickedness result only in the triumph of virtue. The angels need only back away a short distance and peek through gaps in the thick fumes as they vanish. "What? But look! Those two nice continents which are drying up, streaming with milk, all fringed with fringes and penetrated by penetrations, and all escorted to meet the sun in the sea of a multitude of altars! And look at those mountains! They are the very mountains which the Evil One—an Evil One who does not always merit his nickname—wanted to use as a rampart!" The angels point them out to God. In the religious balances they have become, during the solemn breathings of the atmosphere, the ever-flowing breasts of his beloved paradise! They are worth turning to the manager with a smile to ask Him if He is happy and intoning Psalm 103![2]

[2] According to Babylonain cosmogony, the creation of the world results from a struggle between Marduk, the male force, and Tiamat, the female and generative force. (Compare the *yang* and *yin* of Chinese philosophy. Greek mythology has many obvious parallels.)

If I were a painter and had a new Sistine Chapel as my commission, I should depict the Almighty as a wrestler battling it out with the Evil Spirit. But this match would not resemble the Greco-Roman struggles so much as Japanese judo, where the champion triumphs by making use of his opponent's own efforts.

From the outset—from the very hour of Satan's secession, the very moment when he took advantage of the Almighty's weakness in allowing him to exist and managed to become a negative force—there was light to oppose darkness and good to oppose evil. The devil is not the author of his own existence. Nor is he the creator of anything at all. But he is an usurper, a thief and the fabricator of his version of truth, which is the lie. He is evil because he is not good, and darkness because he is not light; in addition, as an active principle (there is a reason for his being called *prince*), he sets his darkness against the light.

Interruption.

Here I feel compelled to put down my pen and to make room for some ideas.

At the very beginning of the angelical catastrophe, a restoration was clearly in order. God could tolerate no damage to His definitive work. The absolute Being was faced by a pretense of being on the part of something which was not. Opposite the actively oriented omnipotence stood the passively oriented omnipotence which nothingness is forced to offer under the watchful eye of God. But nothingness is characteristic of everything; it was part and parcel of the arrangement.

Here was an opening!

Shapeless energy acquired the power to issue orders. Under the needling of the *Fiat* appeared the paradoxical marvel of movement; that which did not exist was given the construc-

tive possibility of becoming something and of perpetuating itself in a form or through a legible affirmation.

God is love. This is another way of saying: His being is
love. And since nothing is except through a certain communion with the absolute being, nothing is which is not a
certain manner of being, through its relation to God, love.
For each being love is based on difference or on the particular
dowry characteristic of him and relating to his way of loving
God. But the kingdom of love is not like the mechanical universe where every action has a reaction and where every kindness finds its reward. Love in its radical perfection, such as
God had the right to ask of angelical creatures, is not the sub-
jective consequence of kindness or the awareness of the good
which is done for us; it is the result of disinterested wonder-
ment, and preferment due to contemplation; it is an out-
pouring and denial of our selves to make as much room as
possible for the beloved being's need of us. "Breathe me in,"
says the Seraph, "and let me breathe in thy whole being, O
God! Let me translate you into action!" God does not sub-
scribe to the theory of art for art's sake. He is Being and there
is no being that has its being other than from Him and by Him
and through Him. Like the Father in the Gospels, He shares
His "substance" with His children. Not one of them is allowed
to shirk from the accounting which he will ask of each. Satan's
rebellion does not absolve him of his obligations to his maker;
and it does not cause his maker to lay aside His self-appointed
purpose with respect to Satan. *If I make my bed in Hell, Thou
art there,* says Psalm 139:8. Not even for an instant does God
excuse him from serving Him. He will not escape this jealous God. He can always fall back on His "omnipotence"
(which, as we have seen, is synonymous with nothingness).
Amen! So be it! (The word is *Fiat!* in Latin). It is indeed
true, God, that *My kingdom is not of this world,* for it
is eternal while the substance of this world is transitory. But
if this world passes away, it must go somewhere. Its presence

is constituted by My absence, the absence which it wishes to eschew. The creature will not always be *subject to vanity, not willingly* (*Romans* 8:20). God grants "omnipotence" to Satan to work below, but his is an *omnipotentia supplex.*

In the beginning, says the first verse of the first chapter of the Book of Genesis, *God created the heaven and the earth.* This heaven is not the Lord's Heaven which is mentioned in Psalm 113:16. It is a material heaven, just like the material earth: both form an indivisible union. The earth could not exist without the sky, atmospherical as well as astronomical, which constitutes its *firmament,* and the sky exists only because of the earth, which is the focal point of the rest of the text. Verse 2 tells us that it was *void and without form,* that is, the passive omnipotence or "almighty-ness" defined earlier. This—this *lebes spei meae* (Psalms 59:10)—is what the Hindus call *Prakriti* and the Assyrians *Tiamat.* For surely God who is the Alpha and the Omega was at the beginning with primordial energy as He will be at the end with the result which He knows. And in the interval Isaiah was to see *a plan graven in the hands of the Eternal and walls continually before him* (49:16). *Lift up thine eyes round about and behold: all these gather themselves together and come to thee. As I live! saith the Lord, thou shalt surely clothe thee as a bride* (18). God exists and His creature exists; but God speaks to her through His many-colored screen of administrative powers; both the bad and the good know what He wishes.

Here, I had first thought of using the photographic plate to draw a comparison, but had to abandon the notion as wholly unsatisfactory. The Book of Genesis does not say that God created complete sets of animal and vegetable species. He ordered the earth and the water to *produce* them for him. There is conception and engenderment. There is a soul of some sort buried deep in matter. This soul, in the name of the divine lover, is allowed to conceive, to think, to propose, to elaborate whatever is required of it. For those reasons I prefer to turn to myths, either the myth of Prakriti or the myth of Tiamat. I am not thinking of hands shaping clay but rather of the bosom of woman and the cerebro-spinal column of the poet. God made a great show of giving himself over to this flesh through his angels, the good and the bad; this tribe of powers, *exousiai*, was prepared for give-and-take discussion. This was the war whose vicissitudes and progress were a part of Creation.

Tiamat stood there watching and devouring everything. She set down, and interpreted. She never stopped making proposals. The great battle between good and evil was high above her. She was down below, on the earth, to stage and produce it. The billboard never stopped changing. The cast was endless. A tireless audience was there, watching. Beyond the prompter's pit was something for everybody. Everything that happened was ambivalent, depending, we might say, on the point of view. The angels applauded and the devil rubbed his hands. But the master of the show never lost his sense of direction. None of the performance failed to serve Him. And at the last scene of Act V stood the Cross.

End of the interruption.

I continue.

At this point two propositions worth considering come to mind. The first is that physical and moral evil are the mirrored likenesses of each other. The second is that the cosmic God and the God of the Gospels are really one and the same personage. A being with his own pattern of being and, as we say of a recognized artist, his own style or touch, in spiritual matters and in matters of the heart. Someone who is eminently good, goodness personified, and who likes to put his goodness to absolute use by utilizing the services of those whom this goodness serves.

So far, so good. There stood the family Head who, as in the

parable, *shared his substance* with the wayward son. Movement, which is essentially flight, had no place in God; it derived from Satan. The devil could flee from God but not from himself, and thus was caught by the tail in a contradiction: the back-and-forth movement known as vibration and the circle known as gravitation which is the generatrix of form. The tireless globe itself was condemned to eternal escaping under the gaze of the Creator. The Creator could scarcely have refused to give His rival the means of seeing and verifying the fact that escaping serves him only in that it denies escape and that His work *was good*. Good indeed! But not at all as he might have thought and wished!

And so it was, all during the Six Days. The devil was not able to create but only to introduce—let us say "submit"—proposals for the huge undertaking in which he was an interested party. On this subject there are suggestive passages in the Book of Job and in the Book of Kings. In one way or another, the dark servant was hired by the day and struggled along at the expense of the foreman only to reach and unroll the carpet on which was to walk forth the son of David. Of what use to Satan was his darkness which, now that it was called *night*, served only to define day? What did it profit him to obtain something compact and solid and fairly impervious to sight —the earth, in short—when it was only a revolving stool under the feet of the Almighty? The air, the sea, the waters, all the physical and geographical wiles at his disposal were not enough to give life to the secession, to finance competition, or to make it possible for him to refuse to throw his weight behind the cosmic task. "Divide" says Genesis over and over. But was dividing not the work of this heretic? What about the continent that was rent from top to bottom like the garment of the High Priest with its northern and southern parts held together by only a thread? And the sea! What a way for the rebel son to spit in the face of his Father and mull over his wrath and tell Him what he thought of him

and hide in unctuous silence in the abyss! And the mountains! "I have at my disposal every size and shape of protest
and insult," said the demon. "Every possible socle which
Prometheus could call upon for support, not to mention the
shadows that they cast or all the pitfalls and means of plunder
and terror that they afford!" He did not have to mention
their capital role in Luciferian politics, which is to divide
and rule. And night! "What a platform for dreaming and for
contemplating all the denizens of space who have a part in
the law to which I owe my make-up, the law of gravity!"

And of course, anything besides God that comes into existence in this world of darkness (*tenebrarum harum*) must derive its existence from Him who gives it His substance and
through Him who gives it shape. But as for whatever is *for*
Him, can Satan take the credit? Unthinkable! He who lives
only in the present (how ridiculous the parody on Presence
is!) had a certain satisfaction on seeing the darkness, which
had now taken shape as darkness, change its negation pure
and simple into a formal, outright refusal, whether fixed or
fluid. Darkness—*the darkness here below,* according to Saint
Paul—existed. It had now been actualized but still lacked one
step: to exist by itself, to procure its own means of existence
through its own particular functioning and in an appropriate
form. And that step allows us to hurdle the following Days
and witness the enthroning of the animal and vegetable kingdoms. The plant came and sank its roots into the deepest
part, into the thickest compost of the darkness which is matter. From it the plant drew the limited life—here death made
its entrance into the world—that allowed it to die; it drew
the being under a particular form of the Being which allowed
it to end its being. Here was something which was but the
epitome of transition. It only pretended to exist, and whatever pretends to exist can only be called a lie. This was the
inauguration of the lie on earth, which is the paradise of de-

ceit! This great liar began the endless process of self-incrimi-
nation!

In the vegetable world individual forms appeared, but
there was no more than a suggestion of awareness in blind
spontaneity. The following days of Creation (the meaning
we attribute to the word Days makes no difference) witnessed
the appearance of a landscape which included something that
was no longer rooted to the earth. Something with wings or
fins glided through the air or down under the waters. And on
the earth itself were all sorts of creatures which walked,
crawled, leaped and hung by their tails from branches, and
which used every available means to develop independent
motion. "Here is the animal," said God, "and here is the
soul, the *anima*, which I have given to it. It breathes!" Plant
life breathed, too, in a way; it bathed in the breathable substance and conversed with it chemically. But the animal had
a self-contained center; it had a life-giving heart. Through
rhythmic pulsations, constant repetitions, and an endless
process of rising out of and falling back into nothingness, the
animal earned the right to the vocation laid out for it. This
life-giving machine joined with breathing to form the seat of
awareness and independence. The animal no longer found
fixed inner support but had to move out; this linked it closely
to all divine work. The animal was linked to work which was
good not only in the sight of its maker, but also to the taste of
each interested party; all parties had to put it to the test and
find out what benefits they could derive from it.

Another magnificent invention, sex and reproduction,
further developed the linking function of the animal. Both
existed among plants. Among plants the haphazard min-
glings that resulted in fertilization were scarcely above (but
with the addition of life!) chemical compounds. But among
animals there appeared the first signs of will and freedom.
They appeared dimly under the vague but recognizable form
of instinct, more clearly under the form of love and the fam-

ily. Freedom circumscribed by general instructions. The vegetable kingdom gave God a lexicon to leaf through. The animal kingdom injected, above and beneath the bare lexicon, a variety of syntax, rhetoric, poetry, drama and fiction to nourish Aesop's fables.

Imagine! "Here is the Animal!" said God. And for his part the Devil said: "Here is the beast!" For it is written that the taste for blood existed from the beginning. Here was blood, served to order! Flesh and blood appeared to slake the thirst of the expectant earth. Into the world came love and also, with endless variations and in appreciation of material benefits, all the rudimentary forms of thanksgiving mentioned in Psalm 103. But as an aside, suffering and death were given an organic, sanctified, indispensable place. Only Buddhistic stupidity could imagine that a converted tiger would be contented with honey and bananas. The saintliness of the tiger is in eating as many antelopes and boars as he can and bringing their flesh to his mate and her young. The balance of animal species depends on it.

Too bad if a little suffering accompanies the saintly slaughter. Love one another, be good to one another, feed on one another. Under this guise appeared the great basic commandments dominated by the law of communion. That is how the first form of sacrifice came about: a particular good was sacrificed to a general good.

That is how the broad outlines of the world around us emerged. That is how the *Mundus tenebrarum harum,* which is *beset by Evil* as we are rightly told (I *John* 5:19), gradually took shape. "Tormented" and convulsive landscapes were mentioned earlier. Everywhere these Titans lie frozen in revolt and blasphemy or belch forth sulphur, lava and smoke; these stagnant sites are preyed on by remorse; these desolate stretches withhold everything from heaven. Now . . . *show Me thy face, for it is sweet,* said the Creator to His Animate Being, and this face—the first that exchanged a glance with

Him—was the face of a monster; it was the face of all the fossil monsters that have exhausted every possibility of horror, wickedness, stupidity and hideousness and every trace of heartless-voluptuosness that cowardice could drag out of the mud. And we must admit that creation is still teeming with this infernal population; everywhere around us, whether in the outer appearence of the animals or in their ways, we find images of hell; they force themselves on our attention. And I need not even mention the world of the infinitely small (a label which the devil has every right to reclaim) which is revealed by the microscope. But this does not mean that the devil created these living blasphemies by himself. Creative power belonged to God alone; the good and bad angels had only administrative functions. But Creation was there to bear witness. It is a witness!

It bears witness to yesterday's great celestial catastrophe, and from the first day it was unknowingly called upon to undertake repairs. To clarify my remarks I have already resorted to the wholly unsatisfactory metaphor of the photographic plate and to the slightly better one of Jacob's cunning in showing a striped, half-peeled rod to his sheep at mating time. We live in an impressionable world.

That did not prevent the Eternal from declaring after each successive step along the way that His work was not only *good* but *very good*. It was good because from Him it derived its full contribution to redemption, to the healing of the first breach and to the clarification and glorification of the One who is the Beginning and the End.

It is possible to find justification for these views in the Gospel. In the Gospel of St. Matthew (Chapter 13), for instance, is the parable of the tares: a man sowed good seeds in his field and his "enemy" came and scattered weeds on top of them. The Master explained the meaning of the parable: good and evil were to be inseparable in this world henceforth and until the last day. We are even led to suspect that each helps the other to grow. Moreover, at the end of the Book of Job, which is devoted in its entirety to the problem of Evil, the Eternal points to the awesome Beast. In the last chapters He describes its different shapes and ends with the shapes of the two superbeasts, Behemoth and Leviathan, which obviously stand for the enemy that figures in the first chapter. *Memento belli! Remember the battle!* Remember, man, that the world in which you were placed is not all peace and quiet, and that everywhere it bears the mark and the influence of the Evil One against whom we are put on guard, as if through a final summing up, by the last petition of the Lord's Prayer. Everything is charged with the sign of ambivalence in order that you may learn to earn your bread by the sweat of your brow until someone comes to take his place on the cross and teach you assuredly not to let your right hand know what your left hand is doing.

First came the plant. Then the beast. And finally man.

Man, the king, the crowning, the high point of Creation. Man was no stranger to Creation. He could not have drawn in the *breath of life* which God blew into his nostrils if he had had no nostrils—I mean, a respiratory system capable of inhaling the breath of God and using it. There is no other explanation for a specific overt act on the part of God when a simple act of will would have been enough. God told the earth to *produce* animals; it was quite natural for Him to order an animal to respond to His prescription, which was the holy spirit of life, through man; for man is a true image, a living image and a real living image of his maker. According to a recent discourse of His Holiness Pope Pius XII, this idea is perfectly orthodox. It is what St. Paul means when he says that *The first man Adam was made a living soul* (I *Corinthians* 15:45).

To procure man, God did not begin by making an idol. He is not a Pygmalion who breathes life into still nostrils and sightless eyes.

Furthermore, nothing keeps us from attributing to anthropoid animals as remote an ancestry as we please (despite the difficulty of reconciling their existence with their surroundings). Nor is there anything to keep us from positing several *phyla* of this animal species. We can even credit them with the practice, along with fire, of certain acts and crafts, and with a certain capacity for tool-making and artistry. On this point insects (I have mentioned the South American wasp which uses a stone as a hammer) and birds of paradise have taught us to expect anything. The breath of God, the spirit of God or the special intervention of God is what makes all the difference; this is how our Adam *of clay* was made *a living soul;* St. Paul (I *Corinthians* 15:45) was not afraid to compare this operation with incarnation itself. Here we are of course on dangerous ground, but our position makes us more receptive to the limited, historical perspectives of the Gospel.

In speaking of the poor animals, Job said: *You are my brethren, issued from the same filth.* We should rejoice on seeing the quickening of the rudiments of intelligence, love, sacrifice, and social instinct through the breath of the Creator, and on being able to enlarge upon the thought of the Latin poet and say, without a trace of pantheism: "I live, and no part of anything that has life is a stranger to me. And through me no part of anything which has life will be a stranger to incarnation and redemption."

As I live are the words spoken as an oath through the prophets by the Eternal when He wished to affirm Himself with particular solemnity. He created or procured enduring man, not by a simple act of His will, but by adding a sacramental gesture to that act. To man he communicated his own Spirit, mouth to mouth; this was the Spirit which gave Him life and which His Son was later to restore to Him on the cross. I like to think that this creation was not a simple show of force but an act of charity truly worthy of God; that

God worked, not with an unleavened loaf, but with the weakest of creatures; that His creature was made from the rubbish of His working Day, which St. Paul (*I Corinthians* 4:13) calls *purgamenta hujus mundi, peripsema omnium, the filth of this world, the offscouring of all things unto this day;* and that here nature, which hitherto had managed to procure agents that dovetailed perfectly in the general scheme, had produced, in a reckless fit of lyricism, someone who was good for everything but especially fitted for nothing, a rank amateur at a feast of specialists. It is impossible in fact to imagine a more unarmed being, whether defensively or offensively, for his presence on the stage would have been impossible, from a practical point of view, except for the development of his intellectual faculties and the spiritual crown that set them off and guaranteed his survival against frightful odds. A spirit within him said: "Thou shalt no longer die. Thou art the King. Thou art the priest."

Thy father was an Amorite, and thy mother an Hittite. And as for thy nativity, in the day thou wast born thy navel was not cut, neither wast thou washed in water to supple thee; thou wast not salted at all, nor swaddled at all. None eye pitied thee. But thou wast cast out in the open field, to the loathing of thy person, in the day that thou wast born. And when I passed by thee, and saw thee polluted in thine own blood, I said unto thee when thou wast in thy blood, Live; yea, I said unto thee when thou wast in thy blood, Live. I have caused thee to multiply as the bud of the field. Now when I passed by thee, and looked upon thee, behold, thy time was the time of love; and I spread my skirt over thee, and covered thy nakedness; yea, I sware unto thee (ego vivo) *and entered into a covenant with thee, saith the Lord God, and thou becamest mine* (facta es in animam viventen). (*Ezekiel* 16).

Such constancy is characteristic of God's workmanship. The pattern of His work appears all through the Gospels.

God hath chosen the foolish things of the world (how uncertain the exploratory states of intelligence are beside the unfaltering steps of instinct!) *to confound the wise; and God hath chosen the weak things of the world* (these worms or larvae) *to confound the things which are mighty.* And He even chose the worm Jacob (*Isaiah* 41:14) to triumph over the most powerful nations. He chose a woman's foot to crush the dragon. *In the place where it was said unto them, Ye are not my people, there it shall be said unto them, Ye are the sons of the living God* (*Hosea* 1:10). Consider also the importance given to the remnant, and the superiority of the few by contrast with the many (*Romans* 1:27–29, *Isaiah* 53:11, *Matthew* 20:16).

I must emphasize the importance given to the female, the weakest being among the weak, as His choice as the instrument for general restoration. The Bible tells us that God did not create man and alongside him woman by distinct fiats. He created both in one flesh to show clearly the indivisible nature of the great sacrament of marriage. *God created man in his own image, in the image of God created He him; male and female created He them.* Thus to be the image of God, the human species must have a reciprocity of natures which temporal realization merely actualizes. Man requires woman for self-perpetuation in one flesh. The simple coupling of animals according to the laws of nature became in the human pair a choice of the heart and consent based on reason cemented by mutual attraction.

We note in passing that Adam is the one whom God drew from bestial clay. Eve was drawn from a being already glorified and invested with immortality. She owed her appearance to whatever was immortal about him.

For detailed treatment Moses took from the general sketch of Creation the chapter about man and woman. In the same way as Isaiah was later to present the Messiah to the heathen tribes, God presented the Adam whom he had procured to

the whole living creation, or rather brought the whole creation before him in spirit *to see what he would call them*
(*Genesis* 2:19). God wanted to learn how his elected Son
would use the new intellectual gifts which he had meted out
to him, especially the faculty of distinguishing and classing,
that is, of putting the fulness of creation within himself (for
his concern was with things as well as animals) in the form of
mental species in order that he might *dominate* them, use
them and have them at his beck and call by changing them
into an instrumental vocabulary. Here was the alphabet
which this child whose tongue had loosed would use henceforth to address Him. Here was an alphabet and a system of
grammar, for language could not consist solely of substantives. It is not surprising that the Word took an interest in
our means of expression and in the interpreter's first attempt
to tell Him what he had done by way of discharging the
duties conferred upon him by his universal stewardship.

The noun is not limited to naming or offering up an intelligible holocaust to the Creator by means of the mind,
breath and voice. As the master of definition and the architect of *causality*, it was the instrument which allowed man to
exert his rule over nature. It opened to him perspectives
which were to extend beyond imminent catastrophes. Adam
vaguely realized that God did not make him for the purpose
of doing nothing. He was the image of God; his purpose,
which the Gospel was later to reveal to us (*John* 5:17), was
to work, and this applied to the Father as well as to the Son.
He was to work the earth as he had been asked and told to
work paradise. But for his work, he realized that his strength
alone would not be enough; he had to have a helper, *adjutor*.
Within him there was a source, a fatherhood that asked for
fulfilment.

That is why God led him to the spiritual heights and
showed him the vast panorama of the road traveled during
the Seven Days. "Everything is for thee," said He to him.

And Adam replied, not only in his own name but in the name of all his descendants until the end of time: "Of all that which I have named, nothing do I need except that which is Thine. Between all that which was made for a particular use and this, myself, which Thou hast consecrated in Thine image for general stewardship, there is a basic difference. I use these beings in order to serve Thee. But who will use the essential part of me, Thine image realized through me, to serve Thee? I need a helper, *adjutor,* to help me to serve Thee, to serve for Thee in my own way and to realize in Thy sight the fulness of service and of the image of the model *Servant. Et cum clamaret exauditus est pro sua reverentia.*"

And then God set to work on Adam who had fallen into a deep sleep. From him He took a rib. Doubtlessly He took it from just above his heart and just under the spot which was to be probed again later, at Calvary, by the centurion's lance. A cavity was left at the spot from which the rib was taken. *Vulnerasti mea soror mea sponsa!* A cavity where flesh was to replace substance. And there stood his future helpmate, his active partner, especially engineered by God, in the name of the future, to draw man outside himself. There she stood, she whom he conceived in darkness and in blood, under the hand of God, in something resembling an immaculate conception.

Up to that point, good and evil had seemed inextricably intermeshed. As a result, the word evil acquired a forceful and wicked meaning lacking in the scholastic definition: *Bonum ex integra causa, malum ex quocumque defectu.* Only God can create and invest. His investment was the existence of something which is apparently blind concerning God and which philosophers who failed to see its idea and purpose called metaphysical evil. This is where the Evil One was allowed to try his hand. What an opportunity! Only he insinuated himself into the image and God *dealt* (as a businessman *deals* in cotton or rubber) in reality (in real estate!). On faith and prayer the demon put the mask of contradiction and lies (for there could be no lies if there were no reality). Matter is characterized by being that which is not, for mere movement is no more than transition. But transition is obedience. Obedience implies resistance and resistance implies composition. But composition implies form, and form in every way implies avowal just as a frown implies a face. Multiplicity, which seems to rule out unity, succeeds only in reshaping it. For survival or for persistence in a state of negation, there must be some sort of rhythm; there must be law, which is a written and signed confession. "What progress I have made!" said the demon. "Through my industriousness I have contributed to a mechanism which constantly extols the glory of God! Aha! Did I not see a notion flash through the foreman's eyes? Can I not use it for my own purposes? It is the idea of life.

"Life! I know life only too well, for it is one of the foreman's specialties! *Ego sum! Ego vivo!* What else is in the Bible? *Ego Video!* There where there was nothing, He alone is able to see the necessity of being and living through Him! *Live, I said!* No one could possibly bring his existence into being and live his life other than through Him. No one knows this better than I (your humble servant, Sir) who derive the means of saying no to Him only through Him, which is sacrilege. How can I prevent the written word, which stands in heaven as proof of the impossibility of eluding Him, from becoming speech?

"After all, I am *Prince of this world, the power of darkness;* that should be enough to prevent the written word from becoming truth. Matter was that which is not, for it is only movement, and movement begs to be that which still is not by ceasing to be that which no longer is. My servants have every reason to call the world that is now unfolding an illusion. Every conceivable shape shows an infinity of beings who live the existence obtained from the Creator separately and for the sole purpose of converting it into nothingness. They are all images of the living God whom I can not prevent from being, and who suffer death and annihilation since they are unwilling subjects of vanity; they suffer vanity and suffer from it. They procure life only at each other's expense in a world where death is the prime-mover of life. Life is inexterminable, for it is self-perpetuating. But if life is but a lie, the foreman certainly overshot the mark in arranging for an inexterminable lie!"

Then, in the fossil murkiness of their ignorance, conjectures and contradictions, scholars think that they perceive an animal resembling modern man, and endowed with certain practical intellectual qualities. Since he had a stone in one hand, why not a second stone with which to strike fire in the other? There is a Brazilian wasp which uses a small pebble as a hammer to tamp the cases in which it lays its eggs, not to mention its other exploits. The time had come for the Eternal to lean over the animal's beating heart and blow against his blind nostrils.

God needed only to suggest man in order to produce Adam, who was His spiritual son as well as his image. A new species had appeared. "I did not create thee to serve me for nothing," said God. "Here is flesh of thy flesh and bone of thy bone. Here is Eve. Here is a heart outside thine own to give no rest to thee to whom I bequeathed my vocative power." If I were an artist, this is the scene I should choose to paint: I should show Adam and Eve standing there, side by side, after the newcomer had been split in two by the Almighty's hand. They constituted the wherewithal for peopling and developing the environing expanses.

The devil was unhappy. "What has happened to our gentleman's agreement?" he asked. "I was always given to understand that it would protect me, as a great philosopher will soon take great pleasure in explaining, from *particular wills*. It was understood that all flesh is grass, *omnis caro foenum*—yes, indeed, or my Latin fails me—and that the distinguishing trait of flesh, as of grass, is the law of being that which is not, that is, of passing away. Up to this point I have looked upon life only as the means of dying; now out of the blue comes an *enlivening spirit* which allows this exceptional mud not only to live but to *survive* in a crumbling world. I ask at least an even break."

Thus spoke the serpent who was the most *subtile* of the animals (*callidior,* says the text) and who—because he was privileged to taste the dust of which all things are made and crawl on his belly—was assured of an advantageous contact with reality.

How could his request be rejected? It was similar to a later request in the mouth of the same gambler; the request made later with respect to Job was granted. God had just given man dominion over nature through intelligence, through the *word* which He had given him. Besides, through the complementary being, who was the issue of his own heart and whom He had placed in his arms, God had revealed love to man. It would seem that all this merited a solemn, sacramental act of acceptance proffered by preferment in recognition of a cause.

In a cheerful corner of the terrestial paradise, Eve toyed with the irresistible alphabet that her husband had taught her. For example, s-s-ss. Right away, the serpent slithered along and hissed the most ravishing improvisation imaginable of belts and necklaces and garlands around her hips and waist and neck. At that very moment they were at the base of the famous tree whose fruit the Eternal, for reasons known only to Himself, prohibited them from eating.

This was regrettable, for to say that it looked edible was an understatement.

The tree of the knowledge of good and evil. The fruit of the tree of the knowledge of good and evil.

The Lord did not point out which tree it was. "Thou shalt

know it immediately," He said. "To judge by the way it makes me feel," mused Eve, "there can be no doubt about it. This is it.

"How appetizing the fruit is! And just when the heat is so oppressive! How good it smells! If ever again I breathe in such a scent, I shall surely recognize it!

"Death? What difference does that make? A scent like this makes one wish not to live but to die!"

"Oh, no," said the serpent. "By no means!" said the serpent, tightly enfolding the woman's body and communicating with her every heartbeat. "By no means!" said the serpent as he leaped up to the nearest branch, seized it and held the tempting fruit close to her parted lips. "No, my beloved, *ye shall not surely die!*" And who can say when the kiss changed into a bite?

Ye shall not surely die; ye shall be as gods, knowing good and evil.

THIS TREE

WHICH?

Here are posed two unavoidable questions.

First, what link can any tree possibly have with the discernment of good and evil? Second, what is the other tree, the *Tree of life* referred to in Verses 9 and 17 of the first chapter of the Book of Genesis?

Apart from the power that the sacrament confers on it, no material object is invested with a moral and intellectual faculty. The Lord must use some sort of sacrament to link discernment and responsibility with the eating of the forbidden fruit in Adam's heart. And, indeed, we are told that the accursed fruit had scarcely been swallowed before *they knew that they were naked and hid themselves.* Later, in pointing out their punishment to them, the Lord was but answering their implied expectation.

There remains the question as to why the Lord chose a

tree or the fruit of a tree as the instrument of this primordial sacrament.

A tree means continuous growth toward the fulfilment that age will bring. The growth of a tree is marked by the enlarging of its roots, the strengthening of its branches, the up-thrusting of its trunk and the increasing of its spread. The tree is the product, the expression and the measure of the time represented by the concentric circles inscribed in its trunk. Each year, through its flower, it asks heaven for a fruit. This fruit is both food and seed in the same husk. Afterwards the tree dies and is consigned to the flames.

When Adam wilfully broke God's commandment by pre-ferring the perishable, when he joined the perishable and communed with it for pleasure, when he preferred the earth of which his body was made to the spirit that animated him— then it was only natural that a tree, which asks of the earth only the wherewithal for death, should be the instrument of his temptation and the means of its implantation, in de-fiance of God, in matter.

Satan had triumphed! God's gifts could not be disavowed. Man could no more stop being man than the lion could stop being a lion, the mouse a mouse or Lucifer an angel. World dominion, exercised through knowledge, was not with-drawn. "It is through his mastery of the world," said Satan, "that he granted me a favorable option. All that I needed to enslave this king to me was an apple, the pith of an apple, God's image kisses my buttocks! Yes, an apple was all I needed. With the pith of an apple I was able to enslave him and make him serve me as a servant! Just look at him, the high point of Creation! The Six Days of Creation ended with him; they ended with God's image—the very image that kisses my buttocks! Whoever has eaten of the apple which he ate will have its taste in his mouth—the taste of the present moment which is that which does not exist! If he had for-gotten the good, my triumph would not have been so sweet.

But here now is someone who knows both good and evil and who, knowing good, prefers evil. Fear not, clay. Though He say that thou shalt die, yet thou shalt not surely die! Thou hast not wasted thy time in paradise! This brief moment was enough to assure thee of the whole of eternity with me. The whole of eternity with me, comrade, for having preferred evil. For having preferred that which does not exist!"

Thus spoke Satan, like a beast which sees only the immediate! The match had started, but God understood the game better than he. If he had suspected—if only he had suspected what was to come. Meanwhile . . .

. . . Meanwhile, there stood the human couple, the two mortals driven out of their earthly paradise and given over to the wide world. The board of the trinity was discussing them. Up until that time, the Eternal had expressed Himself in the singular. Now He began to talk to Himself in the plural.

Behold, the man is become as one of Us, to know both good and evil: lest he put forth his hand and take also of the tree of life, and eat, and live forever (Genesis 3:22). And Verse 24 tells us, in fact, that *he placed at the east of the Garden of Eden cherubim, and a flaming sword which turned every way, to keep the way of the tree of life.*

How the questions crowd our lips! The tree of life, according to our text, is different from the tree of the knowledge of good and evil (2:9). But man was given permission to eat from every tree of the garden except the second. *Quid* of the first? Moreover, the Lord's breath made the essence of man inexterminable. What, then, was the role of the tree of life? How could a tree confer immortality on either the body or the soul, except miraculously? And why did God need to call upon a sentry to deny access to it? Besides, if this tree, *planted in the midst of the garden,* as if to point up its importance, were to serve no purpose, why was it planted?

A shrug is the only answer to these questions for those who

take each line of Scripture literally and separately, without relating it to the indivisible whole of which it is a part. For me this tree of life was rooted as a slip in the first pages of the Holy Bible and bore fruit in the last. After budding forth in the Book of Ezekiel, it branched out in the Book of Revelations until its shadow covered this world and the next. It was the tree of life; as Jesus told us, it was the tree of the true life which consisted of doing His Father's will. It was the Cross. It was the wood imbued with the heritage of all the centuries that have contributed to its growth and edification.

As soon as its fruit had been ingested, the tree of the knowledge of good and evil germinated in the heart of man the double seed of remorse and desire: the pistil which only the partner's pollen could fertilize.

The elements of paradise had not changed. Every existing essential was represented in the Garden of Eden. All that had happened was this: there was now an absence of authenticity. No longer was there something pre-emptory to justify boughs springing from roots and roots penetrating depths. Man was released in a mirage, in a babbling of presences. He felt the effects of sharing in their unwilling submission to vanity. He had in his entrails the after-taste of a fruit that he had eaten, and the feeling that only another fruit could possibly heal him. And thus began the search in which he would always be engaged.

The search may take a horizontal direction. *I gave my heart,* says the Book of Ecclesiastes (1:13) *to seek and search out by wisdom concerning all things that are done under heaven.* But the eye can not be pleased by what it sees or the ear by what it hears. We only broaden the catalogue of our ignorance. If we work in the direction of depth, we are told (7:25) that a second depth underlies the first, and we fall senseless, head first, into the pit which we have made for ourselves (*Psalms* 7:16). And if we follow the practice of the Hindu ascetics and choose the direction of height, *which of*

you by taking thought can add one cubit unto his stature
(*Matthew* 6:27)?

All the evil that Mankind acquires in its search for an
edible truth is steeped in the ironic atmosphere of Verse 22
of Chapter 3 of the Book of Genesis: *Behold, the man is become as one of Us, to know both good and evil: lest he put
forth his hand and take also of the tree of life, and eat, and
live forever.*

And yet, truly the tree of life existed; truly it was planted
in the midst of the garden in the sense that it was its root
and nothing grew except through communion with it. And
truly, too, man was not defrauded by its fruit: the very fruit
that his hand was obviously powerless to touch was to be
placed as a sacrament in his mouth by the hand of God.

Truly, at first sight, what a contradiction a *tree of life* is!
Who would think of asking life of a perishable tree? The
epitome of the passing of time, measured by the seasons?
And yet we see the miracle performed each day; each day we
hold out not only our hands but also our tongues for the
fruit that comes from the communion table. It was the tree
which the painters and sculptors of the middle ages never
tired of representing on the windows and walls of our
churches, and which was called the *tree of Jesse.* And truly it
was *planted in the middle of the garden,* the paradise of
Creation. In this sense, nothing in Creation existed other
than because of it; everything in space and time shared in its
erection. God had hidden its seed in the entrails of Eve for
Adam to come there and enliven; successive generations,
embracing the numberless genealogies listed in the gospels,
contributed to its re-erection. Until at its summit there came
as the crowning touch the flower of the virgin, the rod of the
cross, on which the Redeemer of all the work of the Six Days
was raised and revealed.

—But there is every reason to suppose that in the symbolic
paradise (in which the palm already stood for triumph, the

rose for adoration, the vine for inebriation and the mortal apple for the taste for knowledge of all things) there was already a tree that stood for Christ, and that this tree was the sacerdotal olive-tree which Samuel touched to ask for David's consecration.

Verse 22, the arresting passage under discussion, is really the bane of apologists and literalists who are unfortunately in the majority among present-day commentators on the Scriptures. They manage to avoid the outright and painful confession of its prophetic meaning only by saying that there are obvious contradictions on the part of the divine editor. And then—then there is this terrible *one of us! Behold, the man is become one of us!* Imagine! God is speaking! Anything, anything, anything rather than admit here an explicit statement of the Trinity! Then *us*, well, *us* means God and the angels! So much the worse for orthodoxy! As if the same pronoun could lump creator and creatures together in one profession of existence! And the tree of life that stands as a guarantee against death, as quinine stands as a guarantee against malaria! As if the breath of God had not already produced an immortal soul in Adam without the help of the Department of the Interior! Then, frightful scandal, it must be openly admitted that there is a meaning other than the obvious and literal meaning; Verse 22 has a double meaning! It must be openly acknowledged that neither the tree of knowledge of good and evil nor the tree of life had, in itself, the sacramental virtue and dignity that can be had only through the Almighty. Expediency is the answer, apple-tree, olive-tree.[1] When God said, *Behold, he is become as one of Us,* He meant that Adam had set himself up as the last word in separating good and evil and thus attributed absolute value to a perishable being. Hence the necessity of seeking to justify it through some sort of plebiscite of the uni-

---

[1] The apple-tree is suggested by this verse from the Song of Songs (8:5): *I raised thee up under the apple tree.*

versality of things created by the partaking of the fruit of the Tree of life, which is the fulness of Creation. "Dust, thou must surely aspire to gain the crown of eternity, was denied thee at birth, through universal suffrage? But within the outright lie that thou hast become, the powers which I have given over to thee temporarily and which thou hast made subject to vanity, not willingly, are acting in concert, saying: 'Let's move on!' "